# DISTORTION:

## *The Vanity of Genetically Altered Christianity*

Jesse Duplantis

15 14 13 1210 9 8 7 6 5 4 3 2 1

*DISTORTION: The Vanity of Genetically Altered Christianity*

ISBN: 978-160683-687-3

*Copyright © 2012 by Jesse Duplantis*

Published by Harrison House Publishers, Inc.

Printed in the United States of America. All rights reserved under International Copyright Law. Contents and/or cover may not be reproduced in whole or in part without the express written consent of the Publisher.

# Table of Contents

# Introduction

This book is a revelation God gave me to share with you—for the purpose of helping you cultivate the simple joys of child-like faith. You don't have to live a mediocre life. You don't have to flip-flop in the distortion that religious manmade philosophy brings. You *can* receive what you need from the Lord, without fighting others who don't believe the same way as you do.

I hope by the end of this book, you think differently...and not just for a couple of days but for the rest of your life. This revelation changed me. It shocked me into thinking higher. I hope it does the same for you...because you were not created to be shackled with fear masked as religious rationalism. You were not created to be boxed into a corner by doubt. You were created to live free and to simply *believe.*

*"As ye have therefore received Christ Jesus the Lord, so walk ye in Him:*

*"Rooted and built up in Him, and established in the faith, as ye have been taught, abounding therein with thanksgiving.*

*"Beware lest any man spoil you through philosophy and vain deceit, after the tradition of men, after the rudiments of the world, and not after Christ.*

*"For in Him dwelleth all the fullness of the Godhead bodily.*

*"And ye are complete in Him, which is the head of all principality and power."*

Colossians 2:6-10 (KJV)

# CHAPTER 1

# *God Is A Living Reality*

A while back, I was talking with a good friend of mine. He does a lot of research on different types of food. He studies it all out. Me? I just eat. I don't know what its all made of or how its grown, I just know whether it tastes good or not. I guess that's why I look the way I do!

Well, I was sitting there listening to him talk about food and learning all kinds of new things and, at one point, he said, "You know, some of the food you're eating has been genetically altered."

"OK," I said, still listening. I'd already heard about genetically altered produce in the news—but it was what he said next that struck me to my core.

He said, "Sometimes that happens with the scripture."

When he said that, it went off in me like a shotgun. The idea of a "genetically altered Bible"—that we have taken what is true and distorted it and produced something different from its original form.

The consequences of that started ricocheting through my mind. I went back and wrote notes on it almost immediately. When I told my friend what I was getting in my spirit, he asked me not to preach the message until I spoke at a convention specifically for Christians.

"Why?" I asked.

He said, "Because only believers can understand this."

## Believers-Only

He was right. This is a message for believers only because we're the ones that need it. People who are not believers think naturally all the time. Whatever comes at them in life and whatever they learn along the way is what creates their philosophy about life.

People who think only with their "natural" mind can't really grasp spiritual things. They sound completely foolish to them. The Bible says so in 1 Corinthians 2:14, *"But the natural man receiveth not the things of the Spirit of God: for they are foolishness unto him: neither can he know them, because they are spiritually discerned."*

Believers should be different because we've already humbled ourselves before God—we've accepted that He is God, He sent His Son to show us how to live, and He gave us both His Word and the indwelling of His Holy Spirit to be our guides in life.

Still, there are lots of Christians who consider many of the Bible's teachings to be foolish—it's not something they'd ever say, but it's something they *think*. Anything that falls outside of what they can personally have faith for or anything that stretches beyond their personal philosophies of how believers "should" be is foolish to them and sometimes makes them angry enough to fight. Yet, God's Word is full of ideas that blow mankind's "shoulds" out of the water.

I know that there are many principles that I live by today that make other believers angry—but I don't care because I know in my spirit that they are the Word and they are true. I know because I have spiritually discerned them. I refuse to fight but I also refuse to give up what I believe.

Unity doesn't mean being passive. It's about civility and learning to agree to disagree. It also doesn't mean we shouldn't share our viewpoints and discuss them. It doesn't mean we shouldn't have passion about what we believe and strive to help others understand—but one thing we don't ever have to do is fall into the trap of being bitter or argumentative when we hit something we don't all agree on.

## God Is Not An Opinion

So why is it that believers are so fragmented? I believe that the reason why we have so many denominations, non-denominations, inner-denominations in the Christian faith is because of this:

**We've been reading a "genetically altered" Bible.**

*We don't want God as a reality in our lives—*
*we want Him as an opinion.*

*But God is not an opinion…He is a living Reality.*

Everybody wants their ideas and their doctrinal creed to be what *they* want—so they genetically alter the message. If you ask them, "What did God *say*?" they will respond, "Well, this is what I *believe*…" and they give you their own ideas. But what did God say in the Bible?

God always requires a deep stretch of faith. It's never easy on our fleshly mind. It always pushes us and propels us to think higher and live differently. If Christianity is really *real* and really *true*, then we ought to be living it—taking it in faith and asking God to help us as we legitimately strive to *do* what we believe every day.

God never meant for us to say one thing and do another. He never meant for us to strive and do it all on our own—because we can't. He meant us to simply believe...to recognize the fact that He is God and He knows what He's talking about, and to know in our heart-of-hearts that His Word is true in its original form. It doesn't need man's alterations. That's what the main text for this book is saying:

> *"As ye have therefore received Christ Jesus the Lord, so walk ye in Him:*

> *"Rooted and built up in Him, and established in the faith, as ye have been taught, abounding therein with thanksgiving.*

> ***"Beware lest any man spoil you through philosophy and vain deceit, after the tradition of men, after the rudiments of the world, and not after Christ.***

> *"For in Him dwelleth all the fullness of the Godhead bodily.*

> *"And ye are complete in Him, which is the head of all principality and power."*

> Colossians 2:6-10 (KJV)

## The Big Four

Beware is a strong word. Beware of what? The Word says it's these four things that have the potential of "spoiling" or ruining *you*: **1) philosophy, 2) vain deceit, 3) the traditions of men, and 4), the rudiments of the world.**

Notice that the Word didn't say the big four can spoil your *faith* or your *hope* or your capacity to *succeed*. The Word is much broader than that. No, these big four will spoil *you*—they can ruin who you *are*, which in turn can affect every single facet of your life. It's spiritual. It's physical. It's financial. It's everything.

I consider these four things a progression—from philosophy comes vain deceit. Soon enough, that vain deception turns into a tradition of men. Next, it evolves into the rudiments or the "way things are" in the world.

Philosophy has a way of entrenching itself in a man's mind and taking him away from the truth of Christ. It pulls you away from spiritual reality—that it is only *in Christ* that the fullness of God can be found and that it's only *in Christ* you are going to be made complete.

Philosophy can ruin you because it takes you away from the stark truth that Christ is the head of ALL principalities and that Christ is the head of ALL power. All means everything. Head means that He's at the TOP. There is nobody higher. He's over it ALL. Anybody who tells you otherwise is spreading their distorted philosophy and not truth.

Some Christians spend lots of time debating philosophy, but it's not worth it. Christ is nowhere to be found. It's all ideas, opinions, and vain deceit. Before you know it, you're homiletically, hermeneutically, philosophically, theologically "taught."

## Christ or Commentary?

There is nothing wrong with being educated, but when it comes to the Word of God, faith in what is actually written in the scriptures matters more than a man's commentary on it. If you live according to a commentary, you're living according to someone's ideas—and if those aren't based on the truth, then you're following lies. You're listening to philosophy. Vanity and deceit are next.

Let's say the person giving the commentary doesn't believe in healing? Yet, Jesus healed. His ministry was marked with it and He told us, *"Most assuredly, I say to you, he who believes in Me, the works that I do he will do also; and greater works than these he will do, because I go to My Father"* (John 14:12 NKJV).

Now, who do you believe? The *man* who has a distorted philosophy about why healing isn't really God's plan for us and why healing isn't for today? Or, the *Son* who God sent to show mankind how to live—doing the works He did and greater?

If you choose man's philosophy, which is man's religion and man's ideas about what God "really meant" and what God "should do," then you're up the river without a paddle and you're about to take whatever comes downstream.

It's not easy to stick with God when everything you see around you seems to say something contrary—but that is exactly what faith is. It is believing what you do not see. It's what God has chosen to be the vehicle for healing and miracles. There is a reason Jesus said, "Your faith has made you whole" so much.

## Tooth for a Tooth?

I've got to admit, there are things in the Bible that I've wondered about. For years, I wondered why God would let people do things in Old Testament that He wouldn't let us do in the New Testament. I mean, I don't care for all of Jesus' teachings. I think that the Old Testament "an eye for an eye" sounds a whole lot better than Christ's "turn the other cheek." I'd rather take a "tooth for tooth" some days, you know?

Back in Old Testament times, God seemed to let you slap people around a little. If they hit you, you could just *wham!* Knock 'em out! Then, Jesus came up with this love thing, which is the "greatest of all the commandments." I know it's great but some days I'd prefer wrath. Wouldn't you?

One day, I noticed something in the book of Acts, chapter seventeen, verse thirty. It said that God *winked* at those things because the people were ignorant. In other words, God saw that we as a people didn't know any better. But, He didn't leave us in our own ignorance. He sent Christ to show us how to be so that we would be wiser and learn how to talk, act, and treat one another.

Once Christ came and God resurrected Him and redeemed you and me, well, we became accountable. We can't claim ignorance anymore and just smack people around. There is a Bible full of teaching that shows us a better way. Sometimes I read it and it feels like it's hindering me from taking out some teeth, but I know that in reality, it's helping me to live a higher life of love—and let vengeance remain in the hands of the only One who can really handle it. God.

Once Jesus ascended, it wasn't long before God sent the Holy Spirit to be with us. Now, once we accept Christ, the hope of glory, we have access to the same Holy Spirit that the disciples of Christ had. He's on the scene now and He's here to help us.

The Bible says that He has the power to "guide us into all truth" in John 16:13: *"Howbeit when He, the Spirit of Truth, is come, He will guide you into all truth: for He shall not speak of Himself; but whatsoever He shall hear, that shall He speak: and He will show you things to come."*

Notice the totality of this scripture. Notice the repetition of the word truth and what the Spirit of Truth can do—show you things to come. Also, notice that word, ALL. God is telling you that His Spirit doesn't just contain *some* truth, but it is the source of *all* truth. There is nothing watered down about that—and anybody who alters that is deceived. There are no maybes in that verse.

So, when God says that His truth is meant to be written on more than paper in a book, we should take that by faith and take it seriously. His Spirit has the power to write His truth on our hearts (Hebrews 8:10). That means His truth becomes part of who we *are*. He even tells us that we have "the mind of Christ" (1 Corinthians 2:16).

All of this means that we have potential beyond fathoming. It means we have the ability to live a higher life than we ever could on our own. We can be responsible for what the Word of God says. Now, we can't be responsible for it if we don't read it! That's why it's so important to "meditate" on verses. They bring you not only wisdom, but strength and courage, and a way to pull on something stronger than yourself when your natural mind encounters discouragement from the hits of life.

Joshua 1:8-9 is an Old Testament verse that, of course still applies today, *"This book of the law shall not depart out of thy mouth; but thou shalt meditate therein day and night, that thou mayest observe to do according to all that is written therein: for then thou shalt make thy way prosperous, and then thou shalt have good success. Have not I commanded thee? Be strong and of a good courage; be not afraid, neither be thou dismayed: for the LORD thy God is with thee whithersoever thou goest."*

Again, notice that God's Word in you is supposed to bring you to a place where you make your own way prosperous and you have good success. God works with you through His Spirit of truth, written on your heart, going into your ears as you hear it and coming out of your mouth as you say it...but *you* are the one who uses it to carve out a good life.

---

## Religion Comes from a Genetically Altered Bible.

Today, I find that most believers say things like, "Well, this is what I *think*" or "This is what I *believe*" when they talk about scripture. It's the wrong frame of mind. Why? Because the focus is on *them* and what *they* think—and not God, the originator of all truth. We are not the Creator! We are not the center of the universe. It's prideful to think that our opinion trumps His very Word.

So, my question always is, "What did God *say*?" Do you know what? I find that most people can't tell you what God said. They can only tell you their philosophy and they're own ideas about how God works. But, their ideas may be totally contrary to what God has already said. Why is that? Why are we afraid to really *hear* what God has already said in His Word? Why are we afraid to have faith? What is in our way?

One thing.

Our fleshly mind.

Religion comes from a genetically altered Bible. It is governed by the mind of the flesh instead of the faith-producing inspiration of the Spirit. What is real has been replaced with someone's distorted philosophy.

The Bible is challenging—it smacks up against our own fleshly ideas. It ought to be a faith-producing book. It ought to be a book of pure inspiration. Not inspiration that comes out of our mind, but out of our spirit. The Word has the ability to connect with our spirit and lift us up. Our spirit is the highest part of who we are as human beings.

The driving force in your life should be your *spirit*.

Your *natural mind* should not govern your life because it is not what's connected to God. It can get you through the basics of living, but it can't give you the contentment that comes from being in divine order. Your mind is pliable. It has to be renewed daily with the Word just to be able to think right. Otherwise, it spins off into its own natural ideas, which are usually contrary to faith or God or anything higher than the dirt.

Your *body* should also not govern your life either because it is only a vessel, a follower. One day, you'll shed it and move on. So, if you make it the driving force of your life now, you'll live at a really low level—just consuming and experiencing—which will leave you empty, looking for a way to fill up with something.

It is your *recreated spirit* that God has ordained to be **first**. God is a Spirit and so, He wants to connect on that realm. When you allow your spirit to connect with His, the Bible becomes more than just words on a page. You suddenly grasp that it is the power-seat of wisdom and inspiration. It contains what you need to lift-off, every single day. If you open to it, it can clean up your thinking, purify your heart, and inspire you to live an amazing life.

God is a transformer of human beings, which is why He gave you His Word to be the foundation of wisdom for your life. But, what happens if you take His Word and water it down to nothing? What happens if you take out the core message? I'll tell you what happens: religion. Just a list of dos and don'ts and a whole lot of misery and condemnation. That's why most people don't want anything to do with religion.

Religion always comes from a genetically altered Bible. A lot of it is just philosophy. It has no spiritual power. Why? Because the real life-changing faith and real mind-blowing truth has been genetically altered and lost.

It doesn't matter if all you have ever been taught is philosophy. If you're willing to have the right heart and an open mind, and just open your Bible and let God's Spirit of truth within you illuminate your thinking, you *can* be guided right back to the original intent of the Word.

You can be guided right back to "all" truth. And when that happens, your eyes are going to click! *Bam!* You will suddenly start really "hearing" the Word. You will suddenly start really "seeing" what He is saying—and how layered it is and it exists outside of time.

The wonder of reading the Word of God is that it was written long ago, but it also applies to your life, right here and right now, the same way it has applied to millions of other people just like you who have lived and died, and who you will meet in Heaven one day.

How can it do that? Because the Word isn't just "words." It is actually part of Who God is. John 1:1 puts it this way, *"In the beginning was the Word, and the Word was with God, and the Word was God."*

It's a mind-boggling concept, but it shows you why it's so important to honor the Word of God and not genetically alter it or water it down...because when we do that, we aren't just messing with words on a page. We're watering down the very One who has the power to help us change our lives—which means, we're only hurting ourselves when we fall prey to a genetically altered Bible.

# CHAPTER 2

# *When the Word Blows Away Tradition*

The Word of God is controversial. The fact that we even call it "the Word of God" is abrasive to some—but the Bible is beyond historical. 2 Timothy 3:16 says this when it tells us that, *"All scripture is given by inspiration of God."*

In other words, God Himself inspired *men* to write it and yet, as we just read in the last chapter, God is *one* with His Word. What does this show us? It shows us that God loves us and works with us—both to establish His good will on the earth and to help each of us individually. If we alter His Word, we both hinder God's will and shoot ourselves in the foot.

So, why do believers genetically alter the Word? It is because of FEAR. Doubt is a form of fear. So, when a believer doubts that God keeps His promises, they are living in fear. God plainly says He keeps His promises in Psalm 89:34, *"My covenant will I not break, nor alter the thing that is gone out of My lips."* This scripture is so important to me that I had it inscribed on the front of my church. My office is on the second floor of the main ministry headquarters building and I regularly look out of my window and read this powerful verse inscribed on my church.

One of the most controversial subjects that divide believers today is healing. Some people believe God heals, others don't—and sometimes the ones who don't believe have a real problem with those who do. It shouldn't be that way. Man, I'd rather someone pray for me and believe the best than just immediately condemn me to die! To me, believing in healing is just plain merciful. Since Jesus did it and we are disciples after His teachings, why not believe?

If there is one statement that stands out in my mind as most used to distort the principle, it's this…

"Well, you know, you can't expect God to heal you all the time because you know how God is…sometimes He does and sometimes He doesn't!"

I grew up hearing that said over and over and over here in South Louisiana…but the truth is that statement is a genetically altered statement from a genetically altered Bible.

## The Self-Defeating "Trying" Mindset

"But I'm trying to get it Brother Jesse," some have told me.

Trying doesn't get anything done! I didn't try to wake up this morning, I did. I didn't try to take a shower or get dressed or get myself to where I need to be, I did! The "trying" mentality is in itself a self-defeating mindset—it rarely gets anything done.

The trying mindset is like aiming for success but, all the while, expecting to lose in the end. That way of thinking is the *opposite* of faith. If you read through the Gospels and pay attention to the healings Jesus did, you'll notice a pattern of Him saying that it is "your faith" that makes you well and whole. He never said it was "His faith" that will heal you. It's your faith. So, if your aim is healing, faith has to replace the trying, hoping, and wishing mindset.

Marriage is another thing that people "try" to do. That's where we get prenuptial agreements from—people who aim for a successful marriage, but expect to lose the person in the end. You see, they are willing to lose the person, but not lose half of their money! Guess what happens when you prepare to fail? You get what you're believing for.

I didn't try to marry my wife, Cathy. I married her. I mean the Cajun Catholic Priest that officiated would not have finished the wedding if I had said, "I'll try" after he asked, "Do you take this woman to be your lawfully wedded wife?" He would have told me, "Go sit your ugly self down, boy. You don't try this!"

I believe that you need to take "I do" seriously. You take her and she takes you—that means you take the good with the bad. You determine to work things out. Unless the covenant is broken, whatever else is broken you both should endeavor to fix. Active love fixes most things. Selfishness and fear, on the other hand, continues breaking what's already stressed.

God told us men that we're supposed to love our wives like Christ loved the Church. Whoa! That's big…real big. Sometimes, I admit, the Old Testament seems better on this one. You know, just get a letter of divorce and go about your way. That lets us have our own way. But, Jesus came in and showed us that there is a better way. It's called real love. Love is not abusive. Love is not manipulative. Love is not bitter or unkind, and it doesn't give its heart or its body to another person when it's already covenanted itself to one.

1 Corinthians 13:4-8, tells us what love is and does. *"Love suffers long and is kind; love does not envy; love does not parade itself, is not puffed up; does not behave rudely, does not seek its own, is not provoked, thinks no evil; does not rejoice in iniquity, but rejoices in the truth; bears all things, believes all things, hopes all things, endures all things. Love never fails..." (NKJV)*

We've got to work on what *we* need to do and stop focusing so much on what *they* need to do. For men, it's basically cherish and love her like Christ loved the Church—so much that we'd die for her. For women, its honor and give some respect. We're all required to put action behind our words. Love is always an action.

Now, the covenant can be broken and Christ Himself gave an out for adultery etc.—and some people reconcile anyway while others choose to move on. God Himself is a jealous God and so, He understands what it's like when someone strays and breaks covenant. So, He gives people the out.

Yet, today, most people who divorce do it because they just don't get along—which is usually selfishness playing itself out to the point of breaking down the union. It's a me-mindset, the opposite of love, and not how things are supposed to be. Again, if the covenant isn't broken, you should work to fix whatever else is.

Jesus brought some serious knowledge to the table. He let us know how things should be. So, when He says that we should, *"Beware"* then we should beware.


## Speaking Is Easier Than Climbing

Jesus said some mind-boggling things. He blew tradition out of the water then, and His Words still blow tradition out of the water today. Go and read Mark 11:23-24 and think about what Jesus is really saying in the first portion of this verse when He says, *"For assuredly, I say to you, whoever says to this mountain, 'Be removed and be cast into the sea,' and does not doubt in his heart, but believes that those things he says will be done, he will have whatever he says. Therefore I say to you, whatever things you ask when you pray, believe that you receive them, and you will have them" (NKJV)*

Now a whole book could be written on that one passage, but I want you to notice the first part of it the most. Notice that He puts the power in *your* court. Will *you* say something? Will you *talk* to the mountain? Can you do it without doubting? The power is in the belief. If you believe what you say will be done, that's the currency, that's the power. Faith is activated like this. Faith "receives" which means faith *takes* ownership.

This is a revolutionary concept. Jesus is basically saying you've got to tell your mountain where to go. He didn't say, "Pray that I'll take that mountain and throw it into the sea for you." No, He said, "If *you* would *say…*" The ball is in your court, not His. Besides, you tell everybody else where to go. Why can't you tell your mountain where to go?!

Jesus is giving you a clue there that getting that mountain to move doesn't have much to do with God—but it's got everything to do with you. Jesus let us know that when it comes to mountains in our lives, most of the time, you aren't really "waiting on God" to come through…He's waiting on you to do what He already said to do in His Word.

People always talk to me about their problems in a way that makes it seem like it's all in God's hands. They're basically saying, "Why doesn't God talk to my mountain?! Why doesn't He move this mountainous problem into the sea where I don't have to see it anymore?!" The truth is, it's not HIS mountain. It's YOURS!

People are incredulous when you repeat what Jesus said. It's as if they just don't want the responsibility for knowing the truth and they get angry about it. Their attitude is, "Well, you just can't! You can't dissolve the mountain on your own!" Basically, they're living in fear and calling Jesus a liar. I refuse to do that. That's genetically altering the Word. While I may not understand everything about a situation, I refuse to blame God. I will not make excuses.

Here's another genetically altered statement: "You've got to climb the mountains in life—keep climbing till you reach the top!" No, that's not right. Jesus never told you to climb a problem.

Look, most people who are climbers are always working on themselves, just trying to get themselves to the top. They remember all their family members who had the same struggle and they hold onto those memories to such a degree that it's like they've got Grandma, two great uncles, a cousin and their brother on their back. They get just about to the top and *wham!* They slip up and suddenly here comes Grandma and the rest of them, falling down the mountain, killing each other along the way.

When they get to Heaven, Jesus is probably up there shaking His head saying, "I told you to talk to the mountain, not hike to the summit. It could've been a lot easier for you."

## "God Is Trying to Teach You Something"

Religion has genetically altered Jesus' words and has convinced millions of people to become mountain climbers instead of mountain dissolvers. They've come up with all sorts of ideas to support the idea that climbing is good. They say something wonderful sounding like, "God is trying to teach you something. You'll learn a lot of stuff as you climb that mountain."

I can't help but think, "Yeah, but you also bust your knees, and you bust your hands, and break your teeth..." When I hear people say that cancer is "teaching you something" all I can think is, "You better hurry up and learn what you need to because you're going to die."

Man, cancer is *not* from God. He doesn't send it to "teach you something." The Bible says that before Jesus went to the cross, stripes were laid on His back for mankind's healing—in other words, He was beaten innocently for that. Jesus is the same One Who said that it is "the thief" (which is the devil,) who comes to kill, steal and destroy everything—but He came to give us *life* (John 10:10).

Cancer is a killer. It steals and it destroys. I've seen too much of it and I hate when people claim God is behind it. That's a genetically altered view of the Word—and it's distorted. If people believe it, I don't fight them about it but I do try and point them to the truth. After all, it's merciful to show the way to someone, even if they choose not to believe or take it.

## *"Give, But Don't Expect Anything In Return"*

Here's another one that sounds holy but isn't: "Give, but don't expect anything in return." Man, religion loves this one because it sounds so pious. But, it's just not true.

Throughout the Word, God promises that if you give, it will be given unto you. Look, God made everything to reproduce. It's the law of Genesis in effect. I find that Christians do believe that. They read the Word about it and think it relates to everything...except money. Man, let the elevator go to the top! It relates to EVERYTHING, *including* money.

The Bible says that as long as the earth remains, there will be seedtime and harvest (Genesis 8:22). So, *sowing* (which is planting, giving, doing, saying, etc.) and *reaping* (which is harvesting or "getting back" on what you've planted, given, done, said, etc.) will remain a divinely ordained principle of life, as long as the earth remains. Why do so many people in the Church fight about this?

## What's the Real Issue?

Why is it that we're OK with giving but not with receiving in return? Why do we read the Word and dismiss the monetary end of reaping?

Is it because we honestly think we don't deserve it? If so, then that's a *righteousness* issue.

Is it because we feel guilty for being blessed at the hand of God? If so, then that's a *worthiness* issue.

Is it because we think only what comes "by the sweat of our brow" is valid? If that's true, then what we're really saying is "It's what *I do* that counts" instead of what *God says* and what *God did* through the curse-breaking, soul-redeeming work of Jesus—and that's a *pride* issue.

Money brings up a lot of issues...and most of those issues have nothing to do with money.

## God Is Pure

Where your heart is, there will your treasure be also. It's not about your treasure; it's about your *heart*.

God is rolling in what we would call money and power—streets of gold and the ability to create human and angelic beings and create whole solar systems that continue to move on in creation mode. Yet, with all these valuable assets and power, God's heart is *not* impure.

God is the purest there is and God is the richest there is. He just decided in His infinite wisdom to create a system of operation for human beings that uses love and cooperation with one another as a path to success...for all of us. That's what giving and receiving is. It's God's principle of love and cooperation for the human race.

*"Give and it shall be given to you, pressed down, shaken together, shall men give unto your bosom..."(Luke 6:38).* It's a cycle of moving things into each other's hands—it's gaining *by* giving. The motivation is love and cooperation with God and others.

Yet, the Word warns us that to everything there is a season. *"Let us not be weary in well doing for in due season, we will reap if we faint not" (Galations 6:9).* So, the cycle takes time. I find that there's a lot of weariness and fainting going on in church. People dismiss God's system a lot because of the time issue...but the principle is still in His Word. That makes it not only what God believes, but also who God is. And that makes it true.

"Give, but don't expect anything in return" is a genetically altered statement coming from religion's genetically altered version of the Bible.

## If the Devil Went to Heaven

Prosperity is one of those controversial subjects that has divided the body of Christ over the years. It makes some believers so mad they want to spit! That's why when some people see me, it looks like they are about to start writhing around on the ground like snakes— they get angry, resentful, looking for ways to tear me down and talk trash about me. They see me as some benchmark for prosperity...

which I like! I'd rather be known as "that rich preacher" than "that poor preacher." Bring on the blessings!

Now, I'd like to say that it doesn't hurt my feelings when I run into these people, but I'm human. It does hurt my feelings sometimes. Everybody wants to be liked. But, I don't let that change what I believe. I don't bend the truth to suit the occasion. And when it comes to Christians who want to attack me over some of my beliefs, well, let me just say this—I understand where their venom is coming from…and it ain't Heaven!

If the devil was a reporter and he went to Heaven, he wouldn't come back with a positive story. He'd complain that the streets were made of gold. He'd talk trash about the pearly gates and the foundations of precious stones. He'd call it ostentatious and unnecessary and probably try to show all the ways that God could better use His resources. He'd also probably say God was too distant, that His throne wasn't close enough, that the angels weren't doing a good job…that reporter wouldn't have too much good to say.

Heaven is over-the-top. If you don't like flash, you might be disappointed when you get there. Of course, God says that every desire of the heart will be met there, so I guess if your desire is a mobile home instead of a mansion, He'll probably meet that desire. More than likely though, you'll just immediately realize that what you considered "too much" on earth doesn't apply to Heaven.

"Prosperity for believers" just smacks in the opposite direction of everything organized religion has preached for centuries. Poverty as a form of holiness is foolish to me because if that were the case God Himself in Heaven could not be called holy because He is most certainly not lacking in any area whatsoever. Yet, to many believers, it is a sacred cow—a genetically altered biblical viewpoint—and they don't want anybody messing with it.

---

## Does Anybody Enjoy a Recession?

Not long ago, a man came up to me with serious attitude and said, "You know I don't believe in this prosperity stuff!" He said it like he wanted to fight. I looked at him and said, "You must be really enjoying the recession. You must *really* be enjoying it."

He just looked at me, he went, "Huh?"

I said, "Man, I bet you're waiting for a depression, huh? Why are you angry at me?"

Then, he told me, "Well, I'll tell you why! I don't like what you drive or what you wear…" On and on, he listed what he didn't like about my prosperity. Oh, you could see it in his eyes, too. It was like fire blazing, just so angry.

I couldn't help but see the injustice of it. I didn't want to fight, but I did want to show him the double standard he was dealing in. So, I said, "Excuse me, why are you mad at me? I'm practicing what I'm believing, but you're not practicing what you're believing."

He just looked at me indignantly. I said, "Now you believe in poverty but you've got a nice truck here and you've got a nice house there…I just can't wait until you lose your house and lose your truck because that's what you believe."

He didn't know what to say or how to act. It shook him up. Of course, I didn't *want* him to lose anything. I don't want anybody to suffer lack. I believe that whatever kills, steals, or destroys is *not* from God because He's the One Who sent His Son to give us life more *abundantly*—and those aren't *my* words, they're Jesus' words. Read it for yourself in John 10:10. Still, I wanted to show him the reality of what he was saying.

I didn't go round for round with this man. I could see that there was no way he was going to adopt my viewpoint—it hadn't become a revelation to him yet, and so continuing to bat away at it would be just like putting the proverbial pearl of wisdom out there to be trampled upon. So, I didn't.

You see, it's not good to fight for the fight's sake, but you don't have to back down on what you believe either. The man was still angry, but I refused to be angry back. So, eventually, he just walked off...but he was thinking when he went. We'd agreed to disagree. Civility in action!

You see, if the news says, "The recession's starting to bottom out finally and it's going to get better soon," believers who *don't* believe in prosperity do the same thing as believers who *do* believe in prosperity. Both say things like, "Isn't that great?!" Well, I admit I just don't understand that. If you don't believe in prosperity, you shouldn't rejoice when the economy tips up. What someone believes, they should at least try to live up to.

So, if you believe in poverty, you ought to be shouting when you lose everything to bad economic times. I sometimes say things like, "Go and live under a tree in a cardboard box, get hold of a rat and call him Fred, or whatever. You know, let him be your friend. Eat whatever people throw in the trash nearby. Go! Do it! Live what you believe." I think you need a good theologian to explain how defending one thing but living another is somehow pious and right—it's ridiculous!

I don't back off because of the current climate either. I'll still believe in prosperity if the whole world's system collapses. Times of economic woe and want don't change God's Word. Besides, that's when we need faith the most! We don't have to fight about it, but we shouldn't distort our opinion of God's Word just because the economy changes. Jesus is the same yesterday, today and forever... He's forever *abundant* in nature.

# CHAPTER 3

# *When Doubt Becomes Truth*

Sometimes people who dismiss God's Word with their human philosophy sound so intellectual that you second-guess your own faith...maybe even start believing that what they're saying might be true. If you ever find yourself in this position, let me tell you something: GOD IS GOD. Man is man. There is a *vast* difference. Believe the Higher Source!

Harvard, Princeton, Yale, and Columbia all put out amazing clergy at one time. Go read their history and you'll see how full of faith they once were. Now, they're host to some of the most faith-less thinkers out there—denying God in every area. Why? What changed? I believe that long ago they got genetically altered and it was done through philosophy.

You know, sometimes man's theory can end up being taught as fact. Through plain old repetition it gains status and climbs the ladder. People say it enough that they convince each other its fact, when in reality, its still just man's theory. It's just that more people agree with it and less people challenge it. Pretty soon, nobody cares about the truth or proving anything. They just care about fitting into the current viewpoint. That's called the blind leading the blind! It's called a genetically altered bible.

When you talk about the Bible while you're getting further and further away from God Himself, then it all ends up being philosophical commentary—and that always seems to bleed into doubt and cynicism about the Word's simple truths.

Look, no matter what you read or hear, you have to come back to the Source of the holy text. Otherwise, you have no foundation. It's just philosophy.

Man's philosophy changes every time he learns something new. Jesus, on the other hand, does not change. He was God in earthly flesh. Hebrews 13:8, *"Jesus Christ the same yesterday, and today, and forever."* So, why doesn't God change? He doesn't have to! He doesn't have to learn anything new. He already knows it all.

You see, to many scientific minds, our world is a gamble. It happened by chance. I agree with Albert Einstein on this one point who famously said, "God does not play dice." Besides, if God would gamble, He would already know what the end result would be and so, He'd be able to just bet on the right thing…and that means it wouldn't be a gamble anyway! Right?

God is so much smarter than we are. Isaiah 55:9, *"For as the heavens are higher than the earth, so are My ways higher than your ways, and My thoughts than your thoughts."* The greatest intellectual minds we have got their intelligence from the Higher Source—God. They but scratch the surface of His design.

## When the Nutritional Value Is Stripped

Doubt is like cancer. It eats away at your ability to function healthily. Since most Christian religion comes from a genetically altered Bible where simple, child-like faith in God's Word has been replaced with man's philosophy, it is pretty much a manual for doubting the very God who we claim to have faith in. That's crazy!

*A philosophy governed by the doubt-ridden mind of the flesh instead of the faith-filled mind of the spirit.*

Have you ever gone to church and left feeling worse than when you came? Have you ever left wondering why you aren't inspired? If you are honestly seeking with an open heart and leave without inspiration, you probably are listening to genetically altered teaching. The real, honest, mind-challenging Word of God has been stripped of it's original nutritional intent—genetically altered—and consequently, you leave with no real taste of Who God is.

Psalms 34:8 tells us, *"O taste and see that the LORD is good: blessed is the man that trusteth in Him."* If you don't leave church knowing that the Lord is good and that you will be blessed if you trust in Him, then you are in the midst of genetically-altered Christianity.

Religion never tells you taste and see. They would prefer to not get your hopes up about anything—because they themselves have no hope and faith in God. It's sad but that's what genetically altered Christianity does. It strips away the fire of faith. It pulls the plug out of the wall. There's no inspiration to get up and move, to go out and taste and see that the Lord is good. There's no power.

## A Genetically Altered Jesus

For thousands of years, Christians have been genetically altering what God said in His Word. For a lot of that time, Christians didn't dare alter Jesus Himself. They left Him alone in His deity. They didn't question His virtue. But, now, even Jesus Himself isn't immune to genetic alteration.

Even Christians entertain ideas about Christ that are far away from God's Word. They devalue Him with speculation about His lifestyle—genetically altering Jesus as "The Son of the Living God" by questioning His ability to stay sexually pure. They can't imagine anybody remaining pure and so, they use their own short-comings as a license to devalue God's Son.

Some even claim that Mary Magdalene was Christ's woman. They actually believe He had a baby out of wedlock. I hear it all the time, even from supposed believers. The world has propagated this junk so much that some Christians actually have come to believe it—to still serve Christ because they agree with His teachings, but to deny that He was ever really pure.

## Don't Lose Your Baseline

The Word tells us to "beware" for a reason...religious philosophy distorts things. That's why you should guard yourself against it.

### Don't let ideas that are totally against the scripture twist your mind.

### Refuse to doubt the truth and swallow their speculation.

If you do, pretty soon, you won't know what really is good and what's really bad. You'll lose the baseline for your faith and end up swimming in commentary, rather than standing on the firm foundation of the Word.

Without that firm foundation of Truth, it's like floating through life on waves and waves of man's ideas—watery ideas that will toss you to and fro and bring nothing to your life but instability. It's vanity.

Religious philosophy is "a way" of thinking. God's Word is much more than that—it shows us the only real "Way" that matters in the end.

## Finding What's Real

When I was a kid, I drank real milk. Most of you reading this book have probably never tasted real milk. You've tasted milk that came out the grocery store—stripped and pasteurized to the point that it doesn't even resemble the real thing!

A glass of milk that hasn't been messed with comes with a thick layer of cream on top. It's sweet! It's good stuff! Nowadays, we think that it'll kill us. We drink milk that's so thin, it's blue! It tastes like water.

Do you remember when you could go to dinner and not worry about good fats, bad fats, carbohydrates, calories, or cholesterol? Man, those days were great! You just ate real food and went on about your business.

Notice that you outlived most of the people that are living today. Why? I say its cholesterol! I'm joking. I don't know why, I just know that they ate real food—grown naturally and closer to home.

Today, we've got a global garden. We're spraying our food with chemicals, shipping it all over the world and even genetically altering it—usually in an effort to keep it preserved longer, so it can go further and feed more people. It's called shelf life! If they can carry it another three weeks in the store, you'll have more chances to buy it and they'll make more money. It seems like they don't care about who eats it, they just want to make more money.

When I hear the lists and lists of chemicals on the same food grandmas used to grow naturally in the back yard, I would just love to ask some of these food producers, "Do you have any children? Are you gonna feed this to your kids? Would you swallow those chemicals if we poured them into a glass for you? Is it all just to make an extra few weeks of shelf life?" It's a shame that plain old natural food now costs a fortune and is touted as something special.

You don't have to be a genius to realize that when man tampers with something real, he usually just ends up messing things up. The affects are always far-reaching. Who knows how it plays out in the end?

Changing the realness of God's Word is the same way. Stripping it of its real power by rationalization is wrong. It may sound right if enough people say it, but it isn't right. The affects are far-reaching.

# CHAPTER 4

# *We Need the Raw and Real Word of God*

There are people who *need* the real power of the Word. They *need* the real truth, not a genetically altered version of it. It is literally a life or death situation.

It's the difference between hopelessness and hope, between misery and joy. Yes, it's about heaven and hell, but…let me get point blank blunt. For some, it's about whether or not they kill today. It's about whether or not they steal today. For others, it's about whether or not they go home and abuse their spouse, their children or themselves—or, whether or not they fall on their face before God and start learning how to live His way.

So, when the pulpits strip away the real and raw power from the Word, what do you think happens to all the people who would have otherwise heard what they needed to create a new life in Christ?

## Not Some Truth, The Truth

Jesus is the gateway to God. He isn't *a* truth or *some* Truth—He is *the* truth. John 14:6 says, *"Jesus saith unto him, I am the Way, the Truth, and the Life: no man cometh unto the Father, but by Me."* I often say it this way...

**If Jesus is the Way, you can't get lost.**

**If Jesus is the Truth, you cannot be deceived.**

**If Jesus is the Life, then the devil can't kill you.**

He is the supreme nourishment for our soul. Once we accept Him, we have the ability to use His Word to transform our minds—to renew our way of thinking so that we can not only talk about Him, but *live* His way. It's a higher and better way with love at its very core.

Everything the Word says we can do and have is because of love. He loved us so much that He wants the best for us—spiritually, physically, financially and in every way. He is a good God who wants to see His children blessed in all ways, but it starts *inside*.

## You Need to Be Challenged

God's Word is here to help you stop your old ways of thinking and get filled up with new thoughts—higher thoughts that bring you hope, joy, peace, and satisfaction. Notice I didn't say *religion* is going to bring you those things. A religiously genetically-altered Bible teaching can't do it. Today, I find it's mostly a soft-soap distortion of the real thing.

You see, what's real is not always soft. Real love doesn't always coddle. There are times for everything, but sometimes you need to be *challenged*. The real, unadulterated Word of God nearly always does that. When you begin reading the Word with open eyes and an open heart, you'll see that it can be both healing and abrasive. It's going to *challenge* you.

You see, you *can* go higher in life. You *can* do more than you think. God knows that you *require* challenging. His Word is full of challenging ideas—principles that fly in the face of "reality" and the genetically-altered religious ideas that keep us numb, bored, and lazy. God created us for adventure. Life is an adventure and faith makes it more so. Without God, it's vanity.

## For Tradition's Sake

When people keep drinking and eating religious genetically-altered spiritual meals, they become conditioned to believe the worst. When the real truth comes, they usually reject it outright because it smacks against what they've been hearing for so long.

The truth is a jolting experience. It presses us and pushes us to get out of our comfort zone and do something different.

Teaching on confessing the Word and using your own inner faith to bring out the power of the Word in everyday life is one of those jolting teachings. It makes a lot of people flat mad.

I've seen people get vexed just hearing *scriptures* about having faith in God—they know it leads to the kind of teaching they hate, so they don't care if Jesus Himself said it. They just don't want to hear anybody repeat what He said in that area. And, they especially don't want to hear you take what He said and start applying it.

Why all the hatred about something that's in the Word of God? I'll tell you why! Because it bucks against their genetically altered idea about how things should be. It flies in the face of *tradition*…

and dealing with tradition is tough because people don't like you messing with their sacred cows.

So, what do Christians do when confronted with faith teaching that blows away traditional church theology? They fight it, of course. They trash-talk other Christians who believe it. They reject it and ridicule it, trying to stomp that teaching into the ground.

## Why the Hatred for Faith?

Why would anybody ridicule another for believing what Christ said? FEAR. Its fear at work—fear of losing the old, comfortable traditions. It's fear of change in the Church.

They say things like, "There go those name it and claim it people!" and "Blab it and grab it!" They actually sneer at the word faith, even though that is exactly what got them saved in the first place.

When people make fun of "word of faith" people, I always ask, "What? Would you like to be called 'word of doubt' people?" Look, if we call Christ our Lord, we are people of faith. We've just decided on varying degrees of application.

But, if the teaching makes you mad, you have to ask yourself why—not superficially but really go to God and search your heart. When Jesus healed, He spoke about faith. He taught and spoke about faith all the time.

Jesus did things that are radical to our thinking and used faith as a basis. If He did it, why would any Christian be mad at his fellow believers for following His lead? Even if you don't want to apply that particular teaching, why get angry at others?

Have some gone overboard with faith? Yeah, of course. But I don't think it's because the teaching itself is invalid. It's more likely that they just tried to live on someone else's faith—and never really developed their own.

People aren't perfect. They're going to make mistakes. But, you shouldn't throw the baby out with the bathwater. No, instead, just seek wisdom from the Lord and hold onto your child-like faith in Him.

You don't have to crush what you don't understand. You don't have to criticize what you don't personally believe. Perhaps you just don't understand the revelation they've gotten on that! Perhaps you don't know how far God wants to take them.

We should all let God be God, knowing He can handle these things. He didn't call us to cut each other's guts out…especially over *His* teachings!

## The Common Denominator

I'm on television in countries all over the world, translated into all sorts of languages. Its funny hearing myself with different languages dubbed over. Some of the translators are great—they watch my lips and literally try and talk 'in time' with me. It's great! I think, "Wow, I'm speaking Arabic right now!" and then, "Man, that's what I'd sound like if I was Spanish!" Imagine if it was you. Here you are, talking but a different language is coming out. It's kind of funny!

Does it cost a lot of money to do that? Yeah, but it's worth it. I get to share the life-changing principles in the Word with all kinds of people who might not otherwise hear it. Did you know that there are remote areas of the world where people literally don't have running water, but somehow they have a television in tents in the sand? Some have computers. It's hard for my mind to fathom, but it's true. The power of communication today is boundless.

I've been traveling and preaching at different churches since 1976. When you've met as many people as I have and been a guest in as many churches as I have, you become a lot more open to the different ways that people praise God. People are the same in a lot of ways but they have different ways of doing things.

Did you know that I have Muslims who watch me on TV? They tell me things like, "We want to talk to God like *you* talk to God. You talk to God as if He's just right there. Why can't I talk to God like you talk to God?"

It's amazing that what attracts the Muslims I've talked to is the same thing that has attracted all of us—we want a real God who can help us...a God who loves us...a God that we can talk to. All I ever wanted was a God I could talk to. But, He wasn't content to let me just live life with Him. No, He is a challenging God. He challenged me to share Him with others and called me to the office of an evangelist. It's not a popular title, but I am willing to take the heat for what I've been called to do.

I'm not looking for a fight, but I refuse to make the Word soft when it isn't. I will not genetically alter the Word to fit into a politically correct viewpoint—even if it is what's being preached from pulpits across the world. God's Word is too valuable.

## Religion Never Transforms You—It Conforms You

Romans 12:2 says, *"And be not conformed to this world: but be ye transformed by the renewing of your mind, that you may prove what is that good, acceptable and perfect will of God."*

Notice that God isn't talking about using the Word to change your *spirit*. Your spirit was already transformed when you received Christ as your Savior. It was an instant change—a rebirthing which dissolved the sin that separated you from your Maker and put you back into spiritual alignment with God. And, if you died the moment after you gave your life to Christ, salvation would be enough to get to Heaven—but it's not enough to live victoriously on earth.

God commands you to be "transformed." Notice that it's not something He's going to do for you. He tells you to do it. How? By "renewing your mind." To what? To His way of doing things. The Word is where you find that out. It's your manual for living life the best way.

What's that transformation going to do for you? It's going to help you prove—or show—the good, acceptable, and perfect will of God. The more you renew your mind, which is your way of thinking, the more you will see God's good, acceptable and perfect will come to pass.

## Engage Your Brain

The opposite is true too. If you don't renew your mind, you *won't* see His good, acceptable or perfect will come to pass. So, it's pointless to wish and hope that God will come through for you. Wishing and hoping doesn't bring His perfect will to pass—you must refuse to be conformed to this world and be transformed by the renewing of your mind.

God wants your brain engaged in this. He wants you thinking His way first. His way of thinking is what's going to change you—it works from the inside out. First, you transform your spirit through salvation. Then, you transform your soul (mind, will and emotions) through renewing the mind. It's those two transformations that lead you to doing—to actually living His way, which is when you begin to see manifestations in your daily life.

This isn't about becoming a faithful religious person. Religion doesn't transform you. It conforms you. How? It usually works from the outside in; giving you a list of dos and don'ts so that you "fit in" to the way it wants you to be. Religion has its basis in experience and sense knowledge—it usually is pretty faithless and nearly always tones everything down to a watery version of what Christ taught.

## The Imprisoned Church
### We're Called to Be Fishers of Men, Not Aquarium Keepers

You see, Christ called us to be "fishers of men" but we haven't done that. We've become keepers of aquariums.

That's what the Church has become in a lot of ways. Instead of reaching out and bringing people to God—and showing them how to live a true, pure faith-filled life—the focus has turned to keeping the fish happy, even though that is not what God taught us to do.

Still, the church is caught up in making the fish cozy. Is the water adjusted to the right temperature? Do the fish have enough flakes to eat? Are the bubbles going in the right direction? Is the little cave and coral reef the right color? Oh, we better not open aquarium up to others too much. Oh, Lord, we don't want to mess up what we've got going and scare away the fish.

That's a genetically altered church! We're not fishers of men, we're keepers of aquariums!

You know, aquariums are beautiful, but actually they are prisons...just ask the fish. We have imprisoned the "fish"! We do it every time we conform ourselves to what everybody in the church wants, instead of opening our eyes and hearts to Heaven to see what God wants—and let me tell you something...He wants more fish!

---

God wants people saved, healed, at peace, and strong—spiritually, physically, emotionally, financially and in every other way. He wants them transforming themselves with His Word so that *they* can prove His good, acceptable and perfect will.

It's not the pastor's job to transform the fish. It's His job to feed the fish, but it's the fish's job to take what that food and meditate on it and apply it so that they can prove His will for their lives. God wants that for all of us.

## Called to What's Big, Wild and Free

You see, God didn't create us to go stagnant. He doesn't want us passively sitting in pews, doing nothing for Him all week long, and just coming into the tank to feel the bubbles and eat a few fish flakes. That's a perfect recipe for conformity—but we're called to be transformed, not conformed.

Again, read Romans 12:2: *"And be not conformed to this world: but be ye transformed by the renewing of your mind, that you may prove what is that good, acceptable and perfect will of God."*

I don't care how big the fish tank is…it isn't as big, free, and wild as the oceans of the Pacific, Atlantic, Indian, Artic or whatever! Church is important and God told us to not forsake the assembling of ourselves. It's a command.

Church is for our own good because God wants us united and we need each other, but it's not a place we go to get conformed. Church is a place we all come together to learn and be *transformed.* It's a place to celebrate God and one another's transformation too. It's where we meet and encourage each other, and get stirred up so that we can go back out into the deep…where the lost fish are.

# CHAPTER 5

# Church Doesn't Change People

Did you know that the world's waters are so big that the whales of Alaska never meet the whales of the Antarctica? The two sets of whales never meet.

One set comes down to the warm waters of Hawaii to have their babies. There, they nurse their baby whales and just eat and eat. Sometimes those babies gain twenty-five pounds a day. All of them are doing their best to develop enough blubber to sustain them for the trip back to Alaska.

It may take them six months to get back home and, all that time, that Mama will nurse but she won't eat. She's just giving out, moving forward, on her way back home to Alaska. She's fiercely protective of those babies and she'll kill you if you get too close.

Now, the Antarctica whales never get to Hawaii. They don't come that far. They come up around the South American area. They have their babies there, nurse and grow fat with blubber and then, turn around and do the same thing the Alaskan Mamas do—they keep giving out, moving forward, on their way back home to

Antarctica. It's amazing what God's done. Nature is truly amazing. We're created to be who we are.

Salmon do a similar thing to the whales. They eat, get fat, and then start swimming far away from their home. They're so intent on having their babies that they'll go from being a fresh water fish to a salt water fish. Now, that's a change. *Bam!* All of a sudden, something inside of them hits and, like the whales, they're going back home to spawn. They call it 'the call of nature' but I call it the call of God—a built-in desire to go back home.

I like to say that believer's wayward kids are a lot like the salmon. They may leave home and go completely against the current, but one day, they're coming back to the truth that was sowed into their hearts when they were young. I didn't say they're coming back to religion—that doesn't bring anybody back for real change. They'll come back searching for their Source. God. Jesus Christ and Him crucified.

Proverbs 22:6 puts it this way. It says, *"Train up a child in the way he should go, and when he is old he will not depart from it."* This is why it's important to teach your kids about God in a real way. If it's just conforming to religion, they may never come back. But, if its real to you and you share your faith with them, train them in the way that they should go—which is God's way, what He teaches in His Word—then I can tell you this…no matter how far they stray, they're going to come back home. God's Word will not return unto Him void.

So, if your kids have gone crazy on you, hold tight. Show them love and pray for them. I don't care how far away they are. I don't care how much they're going against what you've taught them. If you keep believing God's Word, it'll kick in. They'll think, *I've got to go back to where I was born.* It just kicks in.

---

It's God's way. The sheep come back home. He never stops calling to them. By His Spirit, He goes and gets them.

You see, its Eden's blessing in Genesis 1:28. *"Be fruitful"*—always producing. *"Multiply"*—always increasing. *"Replenish"*—use everything you got, but refill it. *"Subdue"*—control your environment or your environment will control you. (see Genesis 1:28) Stand on the Word in Proverbs 22:6 if unsaved kids are your situation. Don't give up.

## Church Didn't Change Me

God transforms people. My father found God after being healed of blindness. There was an accident on the oil rig my father was working on and he went home blinded in both eyes. He was scared. After all, all he knew how to do was manual labor, and so he had no idea what to do next. So, he went home and locked himself in his bedroom.

My mother banged on the door but all he could do was rage and cry out. At some point, he called out to God and made a promise, "God if you'll heal my eyes, I'll raise my kids to know You." He fell asleep crying and in the morning, he woke up and could see as clearly as if nothing had ever happened. That event transformed my father's life...and mine.

After that, my family was always searching for God. We were still as broken and dysfunctional as ever, but we ended up going to one church after another—moving from one religious set of rules and regulations to the next.

So, I've been a Catholic, a Baptist, and a bunch of others, but no matter how much of church I got, none of it ever changed me. It didn't mean anything to me. I just went where my parents brought me.

One day, my Mama and Dad got the Holy Spirit with the evidence of speaking in "tongues" and were kicked out of the Baptist church we'd been going to because of it. The Baptists didn't believe it was "for today" but the Pentecostals not only believed it, they practiced it in every service and tried to share it with just about everybody. They also had a whole other set of strict rules to follow. So, suddenly, I went from being a Baptist to a Pentecostal. Talk about culture shock!

All of the churches we went to had good and bad things about them. They all preached religion and focused on one area or another. Yet, none of them changed me. All I could see were the don'ts—nobody ever seemed to tell you about the dos. Their focus was on the don'ts. That doesn't change anybody, especially a kid like me.

## The "Fisher" Who Caught Me

Later, when I did find Christ on my own, I had strayed about as far away from religion as a person could be. I was a rock musician, drinking a fifth of whiskey a day. I did so much drugs, I went on trips and never left my house. I didn't find Christ in a church like the ones I grew up in…I found Him in a hotel room in Boston, Massachusetts.

Thank God for Dr. Billy Graham, who had the insight to televise his crusade meetings. He was the first television evangelist that reached the masses and I owe that man my soul, because I wasn't about to darken the doors of a church. That man was a fisher of men. He is the reason I am alive and preaching the Gospel today and he's also the reason I value television so much. It reaches people like me.

Now, although I got born again and was completely changed on the inside after I accepted Christ, when I thought of religion and following God, I immediately thought about my childhood. My mind went right back to that old, religious upbringing—which was a complete genetic alteration of the true Word of God. I didn't know any other way to think about God. I was already genetically altered right from the start.

So, that's where I began. God had changed me, but now I had to figure out how to live life—not conforming to religion, but being transformed by the pure Word of God.

## Getting the Holy Ghost for Myself

The sad part is that religion often means well, but it just makes the things of God harder than they need to be. Being filled with the Holy Ghost is one of the things that the Church makes hard. I'll never forget how hard it was for me to receive this gift from God.

You see, after I received Christ, I left the music industry and settled back in Louisiana so that we could raise our daughter closer to family. I got involved with a local church that believed in speaking in tongues and I went to every service possible, as well as bible studies and whatever else they were doing. I even volunteered as the church choir director. I had that choir kicking!

I was saved and living for God, but I didn't have what they called "the Holy Ghost with the evidence of speaking in tongues." I already knew about this unique gift of God because as I mentioned, as a child, we went to Pentecostal churches too, but I just didn't have it for myself. I decided I wanted it, but I couldn't figure out how to get it. So, my wife, Cathy, tried to help me.

## Spit and Bee-Hives

I'll never forget the time Cathy and my half-sister, who is now in Heaven, and her husband decided to pray for me to get the Holy Ghost with the evidence of speaking in tongues. They laid hands on me and prayed to God as loud as they could—man, the spit was flying! A few long minutes went by and they kept looking at me, but nothing was happening.

"I don't think I can get this," I finally said.

"Oh yeah you can!" they said and somehow, they started praying even louder. I guess they thought that if they could just pray over me a little harder and a little louder, something might happen.

At one point, I couldn't help but laugh a little because all the "dadadadaaddaa" sounded like I was back in the Vietnam era listening to Iron Butterfly's song, "In-A-Gadda-Da-Vida." It was just a bunch of words and syllables that didn't mean anything to me. Cathy saw me smiling and got a little irritated. She prayed over me harder and said, "Speak it out! Say *something*."

I looked at her and said, "I don't know what to say!" Nothing would come. No tongues, no nothing! Soon, the praying died down a little and they all just encouraged me to keep "tarrying" which is the scriptural word for *waiting*.

Well, I waited and waited and waited. Time went on and I had the best of the best pray for me. I'm talking about the preachers. I'm talking about the holiest people in our church and anybody else who came to town.

I even had the old grandmas lay their hands on me to get the Holy Ghost. They'd lay hands on me and bow their heads. Their nine-foot tall bee-hives would rest on my forehead as they went to praying, with the bottom of their white, flabby, old-lady arms flapping and slapping me in the face as they laid hands on my forehead. It was bad!

I did everything they said. I went to the altar over and over again. I got spit on by countless praying people who tried so hard to help me get it, but nothing I did seemed to work. I just couldn't receive it. Now, I really wanted it—whatever it really was—but I just couldn't get it. Finally one day I'd had enough. Frustrated, I told Cathy, "This is not for me."

"Don't say that," she said.

"Yeah, I'm gonna say it. It's not for me, you can have it," I said back.

You see, I'd gotten tired of hearing, "Come back next week, you'll get it then." I'd think to myself, "Oh no, I'm never coming back up to the altar for this. You people have tore my hair off of my head, spit in my face, and smacked me with your arm fat...I ain't coming back!"

## Into Listening and Watching

At that point, I stopped asking God for it and I stopped getting people to pray for me. Instead, I started to just listen to some of those prayer languages.

When the whole church was praying together, I'd listen to whoever was around me or whoever was loud. Some of those prayer languages sounded like full-blown, real languages—I'm talking detailed with varied words and phrases. Others sounded like the same two sounds over and over again. One guy in our church sounded like a car, like an old Chrysler engine trying to turn over.

I thought to myself, "I don't think that's the Holy Ghost. I don't think this is right." I had no proof that it was right or wrong, but I just didn't think it was genuinely the Holy Ghost all the time.

Then, I started watching the people in the church. Some of them jerked so hard, it looked like their head was going to go flying off and hit the church wall. Some of them spun in circles. As far as I could tell, some of the people were genuinely being touched by God and others, well; it looked like they were doing a show for the church.

Cathy knew I wasn't going up for prayer anymore but still, when the pastor asked for people who wanted the Holy Ghost to go to the altar, she would just lean into me and encourage me. "You'll get it one day," she'd whisper.

"No, I don't want it, Cathy, I don't want it," I'd say back. You see, I was just plain tired of trying. Inside though, I *did* want it. I just didn't know what else to do.

## Cross-Eyed Holy Ghost Preacher

Man, God has a sense of humor. One day, He sent this fiery, crazy eyed preacher to our town. This man is in Heaven today but he changed my life. He was a good man—a strong and powerful preacher of the Word. When he prayed, things happened because he was anointed. The only problem was…he was also *cross-eyed*.

I'm serious when I tell you that nobody could tell where this man was looking. He could be looking straight at you but his eyes were so crossed that you just never knew it. It was like looking at a lizard!

He also talked a little strange—he'd give a sharp "ha-ah!" at the end of all his sentences and he scratched one of his hands *a lot.* When I saw him preaching, I was floored. I thought, *He needs a healing...there's something on his body.* The man scratched like he had a patch of poison ivy or something. I am not exaggerating. I looked at him scratching away at his hand and thought, *Eughhh! Lord!*

It was a great message, regardless of the peculiarities and at the end he looked out at us all and made a declaration. He said, "Anyone that comes up here right now is going to get the Holy Ghost immediately, ha-ah!"

Cathy's sister, Christine, looked at us and whispered, "I'm going to get it!"

I looked at her and said, "I'm staying here." I thought to myself, *Christine, you're going to get more than the Holy Ghost. That man's got an itch! Something's on that man and it's more than the hand of God! Must be a virus or something, I don't know, but I ain't moving off this pew!*

Cathy looked at me and whispered, "Go up there. Go."

I said, "I don't want to go."

"GO," she said and just about pushed me out of the pew.

I went up and stood by Christine. The man came right in front of me and started talking. He said, "Would you like to receive, HA-AH! Would you like to receive, HA-AH! I said, would you like, would you like, would you like to receive THE HOLY GHOST?! HA-AAHH!" Man, I honestly didn't know if he was talking to me. His eyes were going east and west.

So, I said, "Uh, are you looking at me?"

He said, "Yes, I'm looking at you. I'm gonna lay hands on you!"

I thought, *Oh God. I don't want that itching hand. Please God, let him lay the other one on me. Give me the hand that does the scratching, not the one that does the itching!*

Well, the man threw out his hand to lay hands on me in prayer, but he went too far and missed my head. His hand was just hanging there in the air for a second. I figured that maybe with those eyes, he saw double, I didn't know but whatever the reason, I didn't care and I just swooped over and stuck my head right under where he'd put his hand.

Well, this man's hand came down and touched me and, when it did, I felt **power**. I thought, *Good God, what's that?!* And, immediately, just as he had said, I spoke in another language—a heavenly language.

## A Cup Full Beyond Reasoning

I stopped for a second and said, "Wow" because I was so amazed. I remember hearing myself speak out this strange language and, right in the middle of it, I thought to myself, *So, this is what it feels like!*

You see, my mind was still operational and yet, my spirit was praying through my mouth. Then, all of a sudden, my mind got the revelation and it was like a hammer going off in my head saying, "Wrong, wrong, wrong, WRONG! Everything they told me was WRONG!" I immediately realized that what I'd thought about the Holy Ghost had been altered—they'd made it out to be a lot harder than necessary. In other words, it had been genetically altered.

As I write this, I can't help but pray, "Help us, Lord." We need help to think His way—to stop altering His Word and making it more difficult than it needs to be."

While I was praying in the Holy Spirit that first night, my mind was like a little kid's mind. I was simply amazed at what was going on, how my mind could still think while my spirit prayed. I literally thought, "Let's stop thinking and listen to this phenomena."

I don't know what happened to Christine or anybody else that was standing in line with me. I wasn't aware of anything or anyone around me because the answer to my prayer had come true—I had received the Holy Ghost with the evidence of speaking in tongues and it was wonderful! I mean, it was something!

From that point on until today, when I go before God in prayer, I have a hard time sticking to English. I start out in English but then, as I turn inward towards Him, it just happens. His Spirit comes flooding up out of my spirit, maybe because it's just full.

It's like I'm a cup filled with fluid and if you tilt me just a little, some of it is going to spill over. When I pray, its like that fluid bubbles up. I can hardly help it. It is beyond my reasoning and I believe its beyond human induction, range and research. It's not mental. It's mysterious and spiritual…and it's wonderful!

You can't intellectualize spiritual matters like this. When you do, you end up messing it up because you inevitably change it—alter it to suit your mind—when in reality, your spirit's ability is beyond your mental ability. Your religious ideas can't house the Holy Spirit that lives within you.

Man can't put God in a neat mental box. There isn't a box big enough to house the Creator. And there isn't one big enough to house the human spirit that He created either. He made us in His image and His likeness, and He is a mysterious God.

## Get Rid of Your "But"

All during my childhood, I developed ideas about God that were rooted in religion. I learned some things from the words I heard preached, but all that time the religious ideas I was being fed never transformed me. They were simply conforming my mind to a genetically altered viewpoint of the Word. They wanted to force me to conform to religious institutional living—most of which revolved around the statement, "I know God said that **but**..."

There's always somebody around that will jump at the chance to use "but" in order to genetically alter the truth of the scriptures. They're usually looking through the veil of their experience, trying to water it down to suit the ideas of the day.

Whenever I hear, "I know the Lord said that but..." I want to scream, "NO! You've got to get your *but* out the way! Because, you see, you cannot intellectualize this. It's Spirit-led and the natural mind can't receive things of the Spirit.

## The POWER of Anointed Knowledge

*"But the natural man receiveth not the things of the Spirit of God: for they are foolishness unto him: neither can he know them, because they are spiritually discerned.*

*But he that is spiritual judgeth all things, yet he himself is judged of no man.*

*For who hath known the mind of the Lord, that he may instruct him? But we have the mind of Christ."*

1 Corinthians 2:14-16

Natural thinking is opposed to the things of God. The human mind considers them foolish because it can't understand them. They must be spiritually discerned, and the verse above tells us that no natural man can know the mind of the Lord...but that, "we," the body of Christ have the "mind of Christ."

1 John 2:20 takes it a step further when it says, *"But ye have an unction from the Holy One, and **ye know all things**."* Does that mean you personally know all things? Only when the Holy One is on you—that word "unction" comes from Greek-Hebrew word that means smearing and is talking about a special endowment from the Holy Spirit. In other words, it is the anointing of God that comes on you is what knows all things.

This is why under the anointing of God, such change can happen even instantly in the lives of people. It is God's power resting upon a person and working through that person in order to touch and reach someone else.

It's also why when you pray, especially in the Holy Ghost, and then immerse yourself in His Word that you can often suddenly understand concepts in the scripture that you never understood before. They become revealed to you through the anointing resting on you at that moment. They explode in your mind and have the potential, if you apply them, of changing your life forever.

There is power in the anointing of God—power that reveals more of Himself, not more of religion.

# CHAPTER 6

# *Who's the Real Killer?*

Death is another area where people insert their own genetically altered ideas about God. I don't know how many times a child has died and I've heard the words, "Well, God wanted to take the baby home...He needed another little angel."

I personally believe that God *sends* babies. He is the giver of life. And there is not one scripture that says we become angels after death. We are not servants and angels are servants. No, we are sons and daughters of God through the work of Jesus...sons and daughters who serve. There is a difference.

So, when people make that statement that God killed the baby because He needed another little angel in heaven, they are just saying what they've heard someone else say in an effort to alleviate the pain...and not what has been spiritually revealed to them in the Word of God. It's just that they don't know why the baby died...and they want to say something.

But not knowing "why" something happened doesn't give us an excuse to automatically blame God or ourselves.

## The Killer...is Not Christ

In the Old Testament, God's people believed that everything good and everything bad came from Him. When Jesus came, He told us the truth. He opened our eyes to the real killer—the enemy of God and of all of creation. Satan.

It was Jesus who said, *"The thief does not come except to steal, and to kill, and to destroy.* **I have come that they may have life, and that they may have it more abundantly"** (John 10:10 NKJV). In other words, God sent His Son so that we might have abundant life...not death.

God doesn't "want to take the baby home"—that's a genetically altered statement. It's distortion and it's a lie.

Read the Gospels and you'll see how much *life* Jesus gave others. He didn't lay His hands on people and give them sickness. He didn't touch babies and send them to their graves. He didn't condemn and spew words of destruction. He was strong and told the truth. His purpose was to give life...and He was sent by His Father to teach us.

## Martha's Genetic Alteration

Jesus couldn't go to funerals. He'd mess them up! It was as if He'd just walk by a casket and say, "Get up!" and that person would sit up and say, "I never wanted to be dead anyway! I'm going home!"

Remember Lazarus? Read John 11 again and see how quickly Christ's words were genetically altered. Jesus came and wanted to see Lazarus but his sisters freaked out when they saw Him.

Martha said, *"Lord, if You had been here, my brother would not have died. But even now I know that whatever You ask of God, God will give You"* (John 11:21-22 NKJV).

Notice that she was going back and forth, wavering between accusation and faith—first saying, "If You had been here..." and "But even now I know..." Martha knew Jesus was powerful but she was so filled with despair that it clouded her spiritual sense. She was wrestling inside.

*"Jesus said to her, 'Your brother will rise again,'"* (vs. 23) but I want you to see that Martha immediately genetically altered His statement the second it came out of His mouth.

*"Martha answered, "I know he will rise again in the resurrection at the last day."* (vs. 24) She was intellectualizing. Jesus had come all that way to help and yet, she watered down His words to suit her mind...but the spirit is greater than the mind!

Jesus got right to the point. *"Jesus said to her, "I am the Resurrection and the Life. He who believes in Me will live, even though he dies; and whoever lives and believes in Me will never die. Do you believe this?"* (vs. 25-26).

Notice that He immediately preaches to her. He knows she needs His Words in order to build faith...and He ends this short teaching by asking her if she *believes.* In other words, Martha's faith was integral to her brother's rising.

The next thing you know, Jesus is talking to the other sister, Mary, and the first words out of her mouth were the same ones Martha spoke, *"Lord, if You had been here, my brother would not have died"* (vs. 32).

Right then, it was confirmed. Both sisters were in one mind and one accord. Jesus didn't bother asking Mary anything more because He already had Martha's faith and that was enough. The next thing He did was ask where Lazarus' body was laid.

That day, a physical resurrection happened that blew everybody out of the water. A man who was dead for four days and stunk to high heaven got up, walked out of the grave and LIVED. Why? John 10:10! Christ wanted to demonstrate His Father's will…He came to give us *life* and that more abundantly.

Christ wasn't a killer when He walked the earth—He gave life. That hasn't changed now that He's in Heaven seated at the right hand of His Father.

You must remember that the Father, the Son, and the Holy Spirit are ONE in purpose. They don't have different agendas. It's not like God is the killer and His Son is the one with mercy…no. The Holy Trinity is not schizophrenic. Jesus only came to do the will of the Father and that's NOT to kill, steal or destroy.

## The Reason for Belief, God Wants Us Involved

Lazarus's two sisters loved Jesus. They knew Him personally, were supporters of His ministry and even made room for Christ to stay in their home when He came through town. They were His friends. Yet, even they doubted His power when it hit home. Even they altered His statements when they let their mind usurp their spirit.

So, it's nothing new. The truth is that our human minds can't grasp the true power of the spirit—that's why we simply have to let go. It's a leap of faith, man!

We want to believe that it's always something outside of us that is going to do it for us…yet, Jesus Himself required *belief* in order to do miracles. Today, it's the same way. He preached to Martha and asked her if she believed because it mattered.

He wants to know what we believe too. Why? Because we have a big part in what's going to happen! It's how we were created. It's the way the world works.

God's power is limitless and immense but somehow, in His great wisdom, He has chosen to work *with* us to see His will come to pass in our lives. We must be involved— and we must have faith.

**We're so accustomed to what's false that when we're confronted with real truth, it seems absurd...but, its not.**

You see, Martha stated *facts*, but she dismissed the *truth*. Death was a *fact*, but Christ's ability to work with her belief in Him was the *truth*.

The spirit can supersede the body, just like truth can supersede fact...but it's up to us. Are we willing to tell our natural mind to shut up when all those faithless thoughts comes flying in? Are we willing to put down the natural mind and hear what Christ has said? Are we willing to *believe*?

# CHAPTER 7

# The Diseased Delirium

There are so many rigid ways of thinking in the church that stand in the way of us just following the truth. It's hard to believe that we still have racial issues in the church today, but we do. For instance, there are a lot of people who love God but honestly believe that black and white people shouldn't worship together—as if culture has the right to trump the Holy Spirit.

What part of Galatians do we not understand?

*"For you are all sons of God through faith in Christ Jesus.*

*"For as many of you as were baptized into Christ have put on Christ.*

*"There is neither Jew nor Greek, there is neither slave nor free, there is neither male nor female; for you are all one in Christ Jesus.*

*"And if you are Christ's, then you are Abraham's seed, and heirs according to the promise."*

Galatians 3:26-29 NKJV

---

In other words, there are only two types of people—those who are sons of God through faith in Christ Jesus and those who aren't. All the other divisions are irrelevant in the scheme of things. They are differences that will pass away. So, why not let them pass away now? Culture shouldn't take precedence over Christ.

## What About the DOs?

Years ago when I began preaching the Gospel I ran into all sorts of dogmatic people. Whole churches seemed to be founded on what they didn't do—and the lists were often just plain weird!

I remember one time I went to preach at a place and it was hot. I wore a short-sleeved shirt but I had a suit jacket on top. Well, the pastor noticed that there wasn't a cuff sticking out of my jacket sleeve. He stared at me for a second and said, "You have a short sleeve shirt on."

"Yes," I said, not realizing that he disapproved.

"You can't preach in my pulpit," he said.

"It's just my arms," I said and tried to say more, but he wouldn't let me.

"NO!" he said, "You cannot preach like that!"

Boy, was that guy was genetically altered?! I could hardly believe it, but that pastor refused to let me speak that night. I had to go home. Now, the man wasn't a bad man—he did love God but he had been totally genetically altered. He was sidetracked away from the real message. He had reduced the Gospel to a list of dos and don'ts and showing skin was at the top of his list.

Back then, in the South, this kind of thing was common. It seemed like all some preachers ever did was tell people what NOT to do. I ran into so much of this as a young preacher. It got to the point that one of my standard questions to make conversation was, "What do you believe in?" I wanted to know what their focus was.

Every church has a focus. Some focus on grace and mercy. Others focus on the Holy Spirit or the gifts of the Spirit. Jesus is our common ground, but the Word is full of wisdom and lots of people enjoy focusing on certain points.

Still, after asking pastors what they believed in, most couldn't tell me. It's amazing to me how many times I had conversations like this in my early years of ministry:

"So, what does your church believe in?"

"We don't believe in drinking."

"I didn't ask you what you *don't* believe in...what *do* you believe in?"

"Well, we don't believe in smoking or going to movies..."

"I didn't ask you any of that. What *do* you believe in?"

"Well, I don't know...we don't think women ought to wear makeup."

"Why?"

"And they shouldn't wear pants either...its men's clothing!"

It would get to the point of being totally asinine. Rule after rule after rule that didn't have anything to do with Christ. Yet, rules like these are preached even today.

I think that many of these people thought that they were obeying the scripture in Romans 12:2, *"And be not conformed to this world..."* but they missed the next point to *"...be ye transformed by the renewing of your mind"* so that they could actually *"...prove what is that good, and acceptable, and perfect, will of God."*

Not conforming to the world is a whole lot more about your internal state of being. It's a heart and mind issue. 1 Samuel 16:7

NKJV tells you so when it says, *"...For the Lord does not see as man sees; for man looks at the outward appearance, but the Lord looks at the heart."*

This is why you never read about Jesus criticizing somebody's tunic or sandals! But you do hear him get aggravated over people who acted holy outwardly but were hypocrites, snakes and vipers in reality. You do hear Him calling some people white-washed tombs because they looked great on the outside but were nothing but dead bones on the inside. God looks upon the heart.

That means He is not looking at your forearms to determine whether you can share His Gospel with others. He's not looking to see if you have too much makeup on or are wearing pants instead of a skirt. It's ridiculous to think that God is so shallow that He would stop you from coming to Him because of something external. No, God is concerned with your heart and your mind. When you allow Him, not genetically altered ideas, to transform the way you think, it will always be a positive thing.

## The Diseased Delirium

When the message of God gets genetically altered, it always ends up wandering in its own diseased delirium—it gets stagnated. It gets caught up in its own ideas to such a degree that it just can't get past it.

Genetically altered religion can never rise higher than its source...because its' source is the flesh!

When I look at Europe's history I am amazed to see that in just a little over a hundred years—from 1900 until today—Europe went from nearly 80% Christian to less than 1% today. Isn't that amazing? How did this happen? Well, it wasn't Jesus Christ's impact on people's lives that did that…it was genetically altered religion. It was man getting involved, making rules, crushing the truth in favor of current opinions and politics.

Today, most of Europe's beautiful churches are like museums. At one time, they were thriving churches, but not anymore. It reminds me of what happened to the churches during the Bolshevik Revolution, when the communists took over and literally turned them into museums.

To a degree, that same thing happened in Europe, except it wasn't the government who shifted the churches into museums, it was the religious leaders who decided over and over again to further and further genetically alter the truth.

A church loses its power when it removes faith—when it waters down the truth of Jesus' words to the point of meaning very little and turns God's beautiful message to His people into a list of rules.

*That's* what our intellectual activity, induction and reasoning, and range and research have done—and if that's not vain deceit, I don't know what is. It's vanity to take God's pure words of faith and water them down to nothing. That doesn't do anybody any good at all.

We need simple faith that God can do what He said. When we push that aside, it's vanity at work. When we think we have a greater answer than God's, we are deluded, just wandering around in our own diseased delirium.

## "Naaaa, I Don't Believe It!"

Not long ago I met a believer who had no problems telling me what he thought about prosperity.

"It's wrong! It's of the devil," he said and went on to tell me why he didn't think I or any other Christian should be blessed. Now, this man lived in a really nice house. He had plenty of money. It is always mind-boggling to me that someone who actually is blessed can have the audacity to crush the idea of God prospering others.

Again, I pointed out to him, like I do to many others that you may not like what I believe, but at least I'm *living* it. That man was not practicing what he claimed to believe—he was enjoying prosperity while at the same time trying to discredit prosperity. Why wasn't he practicing what he believed? Because he didn't really believe it! You see, he didn't really have a problem with the blessings of God… so long as *he* was the one enjoying them.

He was actually living diametrically opposed to what he was talking about and couldn't even see it. I call that a state of diseased delirium! It's a product of genetically altered faith. He had heard that poverty was holy for so long that he assumed it was correct. He had heard it preached that prosperity was wrong for so long that he assumed it was correct too.

It wouldn't have mattered how much I explained the Word. It wouldn't have mattered if God Himself came down and read the scriptures to Him about it. He would have stilled looked us straight in the face and said, "Naaaaa, I just don't believe it!"

## God Is Bigger Than We Give Him Credit For

God is so much bigger than we give Him credit for. Just look at the wonderful things He created. Just look at what He chose to tell us was His first creation in Genesis—*light*.

Walk out your door tomorrow morning and look out there. The light you see shining and lighting up your yard didn't happen the moment you saw it…it happened eight minutes earlier. It took that light eight minutes to reach your eyes. It had to go ninety-three million miles, just flying at a hundred and eighty-six thousand miles a second to get there.

So, when you see a ray of sunshine, you're looking at the past. Think about that! And we wonder if God can help us pay the light bill? If He is against prosperity? Look at what He has already done and tell me if it's anything short of abundant—this earth and beyond is His creation and it is amazingly abundant.

We have supernovas that we're just seeing now that happened four billion years ago…and the light is just getting to us. Think about that! He created something that long ago that is just now blowing our minds! We're always looking in the past. In fact, some say that when the speed of light is reached, time ceases. You out-run it. God is amazing. He can do so much more than we give Him credit for in our boxed-in, natural thinking.

Do you realize that if you could travel the speed of light, you'd be younger? Hallelujah! And, yet, we're going to fly faster than that one day…we're going to fly by the speed of thought. Imagine it! Boom! End of the universe! Boom! Right wherever we want to be. That's the kind of God *you* serve. He is powerful!

## We're Made in God's Image

Right now, most of what we know is really just theoretical. There are things that are going to blow our minds when we cross over. The magnitude of creation is nothing in comparison to the Creator. There is a mind behind these things. Light was His idea. So was gravity. I'm an old Star Trek fan and their line is, "Space, the Final Frontier" but I can't help but ask myself, "Is it?" I think God has frontiers out there we've never thought about, beyond space and time.

We have some incredible minds on this planet. People who have figured out things that were thought impossible to know generations ago. I believe that, if Jesus tarries, we will one day use light and gravity to our benefit, to go faster and further and see more out in space than we ever have before.

You see, we're made in God's image and we know how to create. But mankind has gotten to the point of such vanity, such diseased delirium, that we just decide to remove God from the equation. We decide that He doesn't exist, but He does. It's such vanity. It's called secular humanism. We want to *be* God...but we *aren't*. Sadly, this same type of thinking is all over the church community.

It takes me back to the main scripture of this book: *"Beware..."* In other words, WARNING!! *"Beware lest any man spoil you through philosophy and vain deceit..."* People who've ignored the warning and have chosen to walk the road that excludes God always become very vain in their deceitfulness—haughty and elitist—spinning in their own diseased delirium.

## Unity to Reach the Lost

As Christians, we need to shine a light to others so that they can find real hope in the middle of all this diseased vanity—the light of Christ's power that is true and right, not neutered. We need to stop fighting each other over the small, differing opinions that we may have, because they truly do not matter. If we would have just come together in unity instead of uniformity, this might all be finished by now!

We're behind. If you don't think we're keepers of aquariums instead of fishers of men, we have over seven billion people on the planet and we've barely touched a third for Christ. We are two-thirds behind in two thousand years.

So, the next time you think you're doing a great job as a believer…think about the world beyond you and your family. Give God credit for being able to do what He said He could do in the Word. There are people hurting right now who need to find Christ for themselves, to be transformed by His teachings and see change in life—they need the power that He brings…not a bunch of rules.

I love John 3:16-17, *"For God so loved the world that He gave His only begotten Son, that whoever believes in Him should not perish but have everlasting life. For God did not send His Son into the world to condemn the world, but that the world through Him might be saved."* Notice God didn't just love your community. No, He loves the whole *world*. It's time to put aside our petty differences so that we can reach them.

# CHAPTER 8

# *Why, God...WHY?*

It seems like the most asked question among Christians is, "Why?" I often hear Christians say, "Why? What happened? I prayed, I believed, but I didn't receive what I asked for." Some say things like, "I *thought* I believed. I mean, I did everything I knew to do...I guess it just didn't work out for me. Maybe God changed His mind."

*"God is not a man, that He should lie; neither the son of man, that He should repent: hath He said, and shall He not do it? or hath He spoken, and shall He not make it good?"*

Numbers 23:19

Most fall short of calling God a liar but, in actuality, that's exactly what they do when they choose to create philosophy according to their own personal experience verses what God said in His Word. In their mind, experience trumps everything—but I always try and show them that choosing to side with an experience over God is the wrong move. Not knowing "why" shouldn't mean you abandon your faith in what God has said.

## Sovereignty—The Wrong Answer to "WHY?"

One of the biggest genetically altered "answers" for the question, "why?" is the sovereignty doctrine.

"God is sovereign," they say in explanation of why something didn't happen, "He can do whatever He wants whenever He wants to whomever He wants—it's all according to His will." Boy, Christians have ridden this donkey until it's almost dead! It's so common. It sounds so good. "God is sovereign" seems to easily explain away the unexplainable. The problem is, the doctrine they use this word to support just isn't *true*. It's genetically altered.

Yes, God *is* sovereign—that's a one hundred percent true statement—but He's only sovereign *outside* of His Word. In other words, God is **not** a liar. Go and read Numbers 23:19 again and see for yourself. Even if He technically *could* lie, He's already promised that He never will. He told us so when He said, *"My covenant will I not break, nor alter the thing that goes out of My lips"* (Psalm 89:34).

God does not say one thing (in His Word) and do another (in life). If experience doesn't match up the Word, God and His "will" aren't the problem.

## But What About Healing?

Healing is an area this is used a lot. But, you can't say "God is sovereign" to explain why someone didn't get healed. God's sovereignty doesn't apply to healing because His Word already tells you that He is pro-healing—and that Christ's work on the cross included a provision for healing.

Isaiah 53:5 says, *"But He was wounded for our transgressions, He was bruised for our iniquities: the chastisement of our peace was upon Him; and with His stripes we are healed."*

So, with His stripes—the beat-marks left on His flesh before His crucifixion—we *are* healed. In other words, the Bible's *"are healed"* is supposed to change the body's "am sick."

This means that, to God, Christ paid the price for healing before anyone got sick at all. How can that be? Because Jesus is the Lamb slain *before* the foundation of the world—redemption and all its provisions are timeless and they're for everyone who believes.

The Word of God is full of the kinds of statements that reveal the truly timeless nature of God—notice them when you come across them in the Bible. Those scriptures boggle the *mind* because they were written for the *spirit.* Go ahead and think them over. Let them boggle your mind for a little bit. They'll expand your view of God.

You know, God is so far above and beyond *time.* You are too. Your spirit is going to live forever. Anything that happens here isn't going to happen forever. Nothing can ever kill you, really. You are timeless.

Your human mind thinks in a linear pattern because that's all it's seen—but as believers, God requires us to break that mental barrier...to speak the future into existence or as the Word says, to *"calleth those things that **be not** as though they **were"*** (Romans 4:17).

In other words, God challenges us to stop thinking the same old way and start thinking the "faith" way. Why? Because that's how He thinks. That's how He works. He speaks and things *are!*

You see, getting a revelation of God's power helps you to stick to believing in His Word. You must get to a point in your mind that God's Word out-ranks your human experience. It is totally unfair to blame God for not getting healed by using, "God is sovereign." It is like saying, "He chose not to heal me this time" when the Bible plainly says Christ's stripes provided healing.

We may not understand why healing didn't manifest but that doesn't give us the right to accuse God of not doing His part or of being a liar. We serve a good God. When things don't go the way we want, we shouldn't genetically alter His Word to suit the situation. His Word is holy. He is God and, as Luke 21:33 says, *"Heaven and earth shall pass away: but My words shall not pass away."*

God's Word will remain forever but our experience will pass away because, one day, we'll understand ALL the how's and why's about it. In other words, if it didn't "work" for you, it isn't that the *Word* didn't work; it's that you don't have the full picture yet. But, one day you will. Still, you don't have to wait until you're dead to know some things about your situation and maybe even, all things, if you're willing to search concerning them.

God doesn't want us in the dark. He wouldn't have given us His Son, His Word, and His Holy Spirit if He didn't want us to know the answers. We can gain understanding by seeking and refusing to give up.

## The Power of Persistence

*"Ask, and it shall be given you; seek, and ye shall find; knock, and it shall be opened unto you:*

*"For every one that asketh receiveth; and he that seeketh findeth; and to him that knocketh it shall be opened.*

*"Or what man is there of you, whom if his son ask bread, will he give him a stone?"*

Matthew 7:7-9

So, when you're looking for answers, you have to ask yourself... are you asking the right Person? Are you asking the right question? Are you seeking in the right place? Are you seeking to really know the right answer? Are you knocking on the right door? Have you knocked once and given up and walked away? Or are you still open to hear and see what's on the other side of that problem?

In other words, are you willing to be *persistent* in your quest for whatever it is that you want and need?

Never forget the woman with the issue of blood in Mark 5:25-34—that woman was persistent in asking and seeking. It was her very faith and persistence that actually *drew* virtue out of Christ. Think about that. She pulled virtue out of Jesus!

Jesus didn't give her anything. He didn't lay hands on her. He didn't pray. He didn't even look at her on the street. No, *she* did the pursuing. She did the asking, seeking, and knocking. *Her* faith made her whole...but *persistence* is what got her to Christ. He was the answer to the question and the object of the search. Jesus was the miracle on the other side of the door she was knocking upon.

If this woman was alive today and chose *not* to be persistent, and if she died with that issue of blood, guess what would be said? Genetically-altered Christians everywhere would say, "Well, you know, God is sovereign. I guess it wasn't His will to heal this time."

It's one of the most common answers Christians give when healing doesn't come or people die after being prayed for. But just because it's common doesn't make it right. It's the wrong answer.... every single time.

Jesus said, *"The thief cometh not, but for to steal, and to kill, and to destroy: I am come that they might have life, and that they might have it more abundantly"* (John 10:10). Those words are Christ's words—whatever steals, kills, and destroys is **not** Christ's will.

---

His will is life and that more abundantly. His will for our health is forever going to be linked to the price He paid, "... *and with His stripes we are healed." Isaiah 53:5*

So, if God has chosen to say that He won't break His promises (Psalm 89:34) and if He has told us that He is not a liar (Numbers 23:19), that can only mean that He remains forever bound to His Word.

His Word literally *is* His will for all of us. What He has said, He means. So, the "disconnect" can't be with Him, it must be with something or someone else.

I like to put it this way, "Either God's lying or you're lying...I pick you!" If you've been guilty of it, stop using genetically altered statements to blame God. There are many things that can complicate healing—but His sovereign will is not one of them.

## What IS a Sovereign Act of God?

What is a sovereign act of God? It's anything God chooses to say or do that lies outside of what He's already said or promised to do in His Word. For a biblical example, think about the story in Acts nine about Paul the Apostle on the road to Damascus.

This was before he was called Paul, when he was called Saul and still an unbeliever. He was a rough man. His life was literally consumed with threatening and persecuting new Christians—he spent his days slaughtering them and his will was only to do more killing. He was filled with hatred and rage.

On the road to Damascus, the Lord does a sovereign thing. Something He never promised He would do in His Word. The Lord appears to Paul on the road to Damascus and the power of His presence physically knocked Paul off his donkey. The man was on the street, knocked to his knees when he saw light shine all around him and he heard the voice of the Lord Himself saying, "Why are you persecuting me?!"

Now, *that's* a sovereign act of God! Think about it. God never promised in His Word that He would come down and physically intervene in our lives. He never promised He would shine lights around us while we're walking down the road, knock us to our knees with His power, and ask us why we're doing what we're doing. But, in this instance with Paul, the Lord did exactly that!

Christ wanted Paul to stop. He wanted him to know Who he was really persecuting. In other words, "Paul, when you touch my kids, you touch Me! So, stop and do what I tell you to do!"

There's nothing else to call that encounter but a *sovereign* act of God. Of course, you know what happened and if you don't, read the Word and see for yourself because it is an amazing testimony. Paul, a killer of Christians, totally turns his life around in the opposite direction. He becomes a great disciple of Christ and eventually authors two thirds of the New Testament.

Paul's life shows us that God can use anybody, even a former killer of Christians to get His work and will done. Notice that, with God, your past does not have to dictate your future.

## Honoring the Real Jesus

Today, people have made Christ an icon of Christianity—but the truth is that Jesus wasn't as interested in religion as He was people. His teachings superseded religion. In fact, that's what got Him in trouble with the religious hierarchy of His day. Jesus didn't seek to abolish tradition. He was faithful. But, He also wasn't afraid to buck tradition in order to help somebody or establish truth on the earth. The heart issue was more important than the legalities of doctrine.

Jesus was not a normal man. He wasn't a sage or a guru either. Jesus was THE Son of God. He was God, inhabiting physical form, and in just *three* short years of ministry, He changed the entire world. We still talk about Him today. He was revolutionary and honoring Him is the first way to start following in His footsteps.

The same Jesus that healed, raised people from the dead and taught concepts that revolutionized the world was the very same Jesus who took spiritual form and visited Paul on the road to Damascus.

This is the very same Jesus who drew Paul to spiritual transformation and inspired him to write the text for this book, *"Beware lest any man spoil you through philosophy and vain deceit, after the tradition of men, after the rudiments of the world, and not after Christ. For in Him dwelleth all the fullness of the Godhead bodily. And ye are complete in Him, which is the head of all principality and power"* (Colossians 2:8-10).

Paul knew that Jesus Christ was more than a man—he knew that in Jesus Christ rested the FULLNESS of the Godhead. In other words, in Him was *everything*. Before the world began, Jesus *was*.

Today, a lot of ministers are more like politicians. They don't honor Christ for who He *is*. Instead, they honor the icon of Christianity. They make Him a symbol and yet, they claim to live their lives for Him. It's sad! It's called "the philosophies of men" and "vain deceit." It's called being stuck in the "tradition of men" and the "rudiments of the world" (ways of the world).

So many Christians honor religion instead of honoring Jesus. Living that way doesn't bring freedom or happiness. It often brings the opposite. That's because an icon of Christianity can't match up to the real thing. Genetically altered faith isn't *faith* at all. The more you alter the Word, the less real faith you'll have.

Again, notice the last line of that passage, *"And ye are complete in Him, which is the head of all principality and power"* (Colossians 2:10). So, you have to ask yourself, "Am I complete?" If not, the answer is simple. You don't need more of the icon; you just need to fellowship more with the Man! *Refuse* to depend on genetically altered Christianity.

# CHAPTER 9

# The Losses of Genetically Altered Christianity

So what do you lose the most when you've been preached messages from a genetically altered Bible? You lose your *rights*.

Suddenly, you go from being a child of God with access to the throne and every good thing to a low, down dirty dog piece of trash. You're not worthy. You can't go boldly to the throne of grace, much less anywhere else. Anything you hear that might lift your confidence in yourself is dashed with words like, "I know that's what the Bible says, but that's not what it really *means*" or "Who do you think you are that God would speak to *you*?"

Genetically altered teachings almost always kill your self-esteem—you suddenly become the victim and the victory they talk about always seems to stay in the afterlife, the sweet by and by. Here are some of the losses of accepting teaching from a genetically altered Bible: 1) the joys of salvation, 2) a loss of Christian liberality, and 3) good seed grown in good ground.

## The Joys of Salvation

I love being saved. I am free. I have joy in my life—greater than I ever had when I didn't know God. I don't think about anything I gave up. There is nothing I want to go back to.

When was the last time you saw a happy Christian? Think about it! Have you looked at people in church sometimes? They don't look happy!

A while back I saw a news report on television about a seven year old boy who stole a car. When they asked him why he did it, he said it was because he didn't want to go to Sunday school! The kid had his foot on the gas and was just running through lights!

People gasped and said things like, "He shouldn't have done that" but all I could think of was, *Well, have you ever been to his Sunday school class?!* Maybe that kid needed to flee any way he could! Maybe he was enduring a genetically altered teacher.

I mean, when was the last time you saw truly happy Christians going to church? Think about it for a minute. Have you ever *seen* people's faces as they're looking for a parking spot? They don't look happy!

Have you ever asked yourself why people look so much happier at football games? It's because they're more exciting and they appease the emotions—and so, people *want* to be there. They want to see winning. Notice they don't look happy when they're leaving if their team lost. The goal is to win—to overcome at all costs and get the prize.

When a church preaches a genetically altered version of the Bible, what they're usually preaching is about losing—the focus isn't high, it's low. It's a downer and very few people actually want to be bombarded with the feeling of loss and misery. They get enough of that out in the world, why would they want it in church?

The message of Christ is a joyful one. Your salvation is about returning to God's love, and that's nothing if not joyful. If you don't experience joy from it, perhaps you've been enduring too much genetically altered faith.

As for me, I prefer to live with the original joy of my salvation. I refuse to be bound by religion—what man thinks I ought to feel like, do, and have in life. No, God made a way for me to have joy, live by faith, and enjoy life and all of its abundance.

You see, my mind isn't on loss...it's on benefits. There are so many benefits to salvation—things like peace that passes all understanding, living in the blessing, walking in faith that stagger the average person's thinking. It's the kind of faith that changes not only the way I think, but the physical world around me.

I love to stretch my thinking. I love to apply my faith. I mean, just think about biblically taught benefits like healing, the hundred fold return, and the most important thing of all, *access* to God Almighty. Living with these things not only makes my life better, it makes the world a better place for me to live—because what I bring to each day affects others. My faith stimulates other's to have faith.

That's what letting your light shine is all about. Joy is contagious. It beats sadness any day of the week. Hold on to the joys of your salvation. Refuse to let genetically altered teaching steal joy from your life. You need it too much...and the world around you needs it too.

## A Loss of Christian Liberality

Another thing that teachings from a genetically altered bible cause you to lose is Christian liberality. Man, if you want to feel like you're in bondage, just become a typical Christian in a typical American church. You can't show excitement. You better not shout. You're allowed to pray but quietly and with the assumption that it might not do any good anyway because "you never know what God's going to do." You might as well get your dice out because "you know how God is...sometimes He does and sometimes He doesn't." I call it the Christian casino. It's if prayer is a gamble.

That's why when a true miracle happens, people just about lose their minds in awe. In reality, we *shouldn't* get all that excited because it ought to be a regular occurrence. The God we serve ought to do what He says, right? Well, I believe that He is always doing what He said He would do in His Word...but maybe the reason we're not receiving is because we're not really reading His Word and so, we don't really apply it.

Our minds are often so locked in on the problem that we become totally encompassed with the ways of the flesh—living problem-minded, when the Word is totally the opposite. The Word is solution-based because it is based on God and He is always the solution. His Words reflect that. They are spirit-filled and so, they are not problem-focused.

When God's Word says "by His stripes, you were healed" it is speaking forth the solution. If you continue speaking the problem, "I am sick!" then your focus is not going in the direction of your solution. You are literally giving more weight and energy to what you don't want! You are literally perpetuating the problem. That totally and completely obliterates your ability to have faith, the very thing that Christ so often said brought the manifestation of health.

Yet, when you've been genetically altered for so long, you end up living in a state of negative emotion. You are constantly moved by your senses. How you *feel* becomes first place, instead of what

God *says*. This is vain deceit! It's living a lie. Its saying you believe and doing the opposite, and so everything cancels out.

This is why people can pray all the time, but in their hearts, they always push themselves deeper and deeper into the problem—all their energy is spent in the wrong place (on the problem) and yet, they're praying! I call that a form of bondage. It's a loss of true Christian liberality…a side effect of a genetically altered Bible.

## Abasing and Abounding

In the ministry, there are many leaders who have fallen into the trap of losing their Christian liberality. They are not free. They think either lower or higher than they ought to about themselves and the work God has placed in their care.

They either think they're so low that they can't do anything, and so they don't ever rise to the level God wants them to rise to. Or, they think so highly of themselves that they start requiring everybody to just about fall down and bow when they come through the church door, and consequently don't rise to the level God wants them to or they fall once they get there.

When I hear things like, "I can't go to a church unless they have at least a thousand people to meet my budget" I just have to ask them, "Have you ever had financial trouble?" They nearly always say, "Yes." I believe that requirements like that that are often why because they reveal a heart issue that easily leads to lack.

You see, God is the Source, not a thousand people or even ten thousand people. After all, God could move upon just one or two people to meet not only the budgetary needs of that ministry, but give over and above to do even greater works. It is *liberating* to have faith in God. It takes the limits off.

There are so many small ways that some preachers show they've been genetically altered. From "Let me bless you with my presence" to "Oh, I can't drink that kind of water" it seems like many have forgotten Paul's leadership advice about contentment and going with the flow in any situation that arises when spreading the Gospel.

> *"I know both how to be abased, and I know how to abound: every where and in all things I am instructed both to be full and to be hungry, both to abound and to suffer need.*
>
> *"I can do all things through Christ which strengtheneth me."*

Philippians 4:12-13

Of course, we'd all prefer to abound, but if I get into an abasing situation, I just hang with it. Why? Because I can do all things through Christ. I figure that, if I've got to stay in a trashy hotel somewhere, so does Jesus. If I've got to eat some crazy food, so does Jesus...because He never leaves me or forsakes me.

Do I wish everybody always treated me nicely? Yes, that would be great! I've been an evangelist, traveling and spreading the Word, since 1976 and, it's a shame to say it, but in all that time the ones who've treated me the worst have been *Christians*. You wouldn't think it, but I've had many unbelievers treat me better, especially in the early years of ministry.

I'll never forget this one pastor who invited me to preach at his church in Arkansas. It was the dead of winter and freezing cold. He put me in the evangelist's quarters in his church building and because he wanted to save money on electricity, he cut off the heat. It was 28 degrees...inside.

I thought something was wrong with the heater. So, I jogged in place just to try and warm up. They didn't have a phone, so I walked outside and couldn't believe it was just as cold outside as it was inside. The next morning, when I told the pastor, "There's no heat in there," I could hardly believe his response.

"Yeah, you've got to endure hardness as a good soldier!" he said and told me he didn't want to pay for the heat. I could hardly believe it. Today I know that he had a genetically altered viewpoint—he thought suffering was a rite of passage and it was his duty to inflict it.

I dealt with this a lot in my early years of ministry because there was a greater measure of suffering philosophy being taught. Everyone seemed to suffer, suffer, and suffer for God. They equated it to holiness, but in reality, most of that suffering was totally uncalled for. It came out of a genetically altered Bible.

When I preached, I noticed that people would say things like, "You are such a breath of fresh air." It was because they'd lost all their freedom…and so, they'd also lost most of their joy.

## The Joy of Salvation—Gone

Back then, I noticed that most of the time, people who went to church were not happy at all. They couldn't wear what they wanted—and it wasn't like they wanted to dress as if they were promiscuous. They just wanted to look fashionable or, at the least, be able to wear a sleeveless dress! Many of the churches I preached at in my early years said no to make-up, pants, and sleeveless dresses. Women could barely show a collarbone without someone calling them a "Jezebel!"

Just to crack a hole in their philosophy, I'd say, "Man, if an armpit turns you on, you need God!" You see, it was ridiculous. It was a genetically altered viewpoint of the Bible and totally about keeping people bound—when God created us to be free. Joy is a fruit of His Spirit. Suffering may happen to you, but notice that it isn't listed in the fruits of the spirit or in the gifts either—it's not even a part of God's nature. But it is the way of this world. Yet, God gives us insight throughout His Word about ways to overcome its sting.

You know, if sin would never have entered into the earth, there would be no need for suffering or judgment of any kind. Remember, before the fall, God's only restraining instruction was to "subdue" whatever rose up against Him or man. I believe that is still His instruction to us today—not to subdue ourselves against sleeves or makeup, but to subdue real evil when it arises.

So, when people spin off into philosophies that steal people's liberality, they also end up stealing the joy of their salvation. Listen, salvation is liberating, not confining!

Many people think that freedom is doing whatever you want, whenever you want, to whoever you want—but that's not real freedom…that's anarchy.

Freedom is knowing that everything is permissible, but not everything is helpful to you. The Amplified Bible Version of 1 Corinthians 6:12 says it best: *"Everything is permissible (allowable and lawful) for me; but not all things are helpful (good for me to do, expedient and profitable when considered with other things). Everything is lawful for me, but I will not become the slave of anything or be brought under its power."*

You see, God trusts you more than people do! He wants to lead you with His Word and His Spirit. Following Him is not about adhering to every manmade rule. It's about adhering to His Word and what He's written on the conscious of your heart.

God wants us all to submit to authority in the church because He instituted the five fold ministry to build up the church people but He never told us we had to submit to *control*. That is what will rob you of the joy of your salvation…because never forget that God gave His best when He gave you Jesus.

You see, God didn't do that so that you would give Christ your heart and then, go through life jumping through the hoops of a man's vain philosophy. He didn't mean for you to bow down to control. He meant for you to bow to His Son. So, look in the Word and ask yourself, "What did Jesus say? What did Jesus teach?"

I promise, you won't find one verse about armpits.

## Good Seed in Good Ground

Here's another form of vain deceit—the idea that as a Christian you should sow but never reap. This is a philosophy of man. It has nothing to do with what's in the scripture, which repeatedly teaches us that sowing and reaping go hand in hand. It is a system. It's God's law for earth. What you sow, you shall reap. Whatever measure you use in sowing, that's what will be used to be given back to you. Reaping is God's way!

Why has the church preached poverty as a blessing for so long? Why have they sold us the lie that wealth is bad and you should give, but expect nothing in return? I'll tell you one reason—it's a lie the devil sold to the church so that he could control the economy of the world and the church. There is power in finances. It's a power that can be used to bless and help people, to meet not only their basic needs but their heart desires! It can change circumstances around in a moment.

You see, wealth is for you. You were created to have everything you need, which is one reason you don't enjoy struggling—but for centuries the Church swallowed the lie that said poverty is next to godliness. Many people today may not use those exact words, but they assume that when you serve God, you should not live well—as if a nice car or house or pair of shoes could possibly be equated to ungodliness.

Many believe that, if you're a true Christian, you shouldn't care about money at all. Yet, God never said that in His Word. He wouldn't encourage you to sow and reap if He was against you being blessed. He filled the Word with scripture after scripture about the His blessings on His people. He just didn't want you to lose sight of the true Source of everything—Him!

You see, money is powerful. The devil knows that without money, you can't reach as many people. If you have nothing to give, you can't help someone in need...you can barely think past your own survival. God wants you to think higher and aim bigger. It's not about just you and your family living well...it's about spreading your blessing with the others. If all you care about is your family, you're thinking too small.

Remember that the devil's motive is always the same—to kill, steal, and destroy (John 10:10). One way to accomplish those things is to make you think having finances is irrelevant to God's plan. Yet, finance is what can help feed the hungry. Finance can preach the Gospel to the four corners of the world—bringing hope to the hope-less and salvation to the lost. Finance is *relevant*. Good seed sown in good ground is *invaluable*.

Make no mistake. Galatians 6:7 plainly says, *"Be not deceived; God is not mocked: for whatsoever a man soweth, that shall he also reap."* So, when someone tells you that sowing and reaping doesn't relate to finances...remind yourself that you are hearing a genetically altered truth. "Whatsoever" includes it all—spiritual, physical, and financial. It covers every facet of life, including finances. That may or may not be popular, but it is the truth because the Word says it. Be *not* deceived!

The joy of your salvation, your Christian liberality, and your seed is just too important to lose to a distorted philosophy. No matter what you hear, if it steals what God meant for you to have, its not worth listening to. Refuse to succumb to genetically altered Christianity!

# CHAPTER 10

# "God's Gonna Kill You, Boy!"

The problem is that genetically altered teachings don't give you what you need to actually *live* by the Word. You may know *what* to do, but you don't have the *power* to do it.

When the truth of the Word has been stripped, the power and the joy get stripped too. The warm rays of God's divine light get stamped right on out, and when you don't have any light, fear sets in.

I was raised fearing God. Not fearing in the biblical sense, which means respect and honor...no, I'm talking straight up fear. Now, I'm not harping on any church in particular because I've been to many. When kids at school said, "What religion are you?" I said, "Pick one, I been there." But, the truth is that I heard "God's gonna kill you, boy!" from the children's leaders at all kinds of different churches...and I believed it!

"If you don't stop doing that, boy, God is gonna kill ya! He's gonna getcha, I'm telling you, He is!" Man, I knew I was bad but I was so afraid of God, there was no way I was going to pray. I figured

He was ready with a lightning bolt and I was better off not reminding Him that I was around.

If I went into the confessional, I lied like a dog. I didn't rat on myself because I didn't want God to kill me. I wanted to live and not die! I figured there was no use making Him mad in His own house.

Today, a lot of people live the same way. They just avoid God altogether because they see Him as some angry tyrant in the sky just waiting to strike people down with sickness, misery, and death. That's living in fear! And fear tolerated is faith contaminated.

Do you know what fear really is? It's a lack of spirit-strength. When your spirit is strong, fear and all it's spin-offs like worry and anxiety dissipate. You radiate peace.

## Don't Deny the Problem, Deny It's Right

Years ago, I had a friend who wanted a baby. He and his wife were told it was impossible because she had had severe endometriosis when she was young and it scared her body so bad, they said she just couldn't conceive.

Well, I didn't know that until they came to our house one day to visit and, all of a sudden, the wife just started to cry. I looked at my friend and said, "What's the matter?" "We want a baby," he said. I joked and said, "Do you know how much a baby costs?!" Then, they told me their problem.

"OK," I said, "Well, I'll pray for you."

"Do you think we could?" they said, "The doctor said we can't have any."

I told them, "I don't deny the problem; I just deny its right." Then, I took them to Genesis chapter one and showed them where

God told Adam and Eve to "be fruitful" and then, I took him to the next chapter where it says, "And Adam knew Eve." After, I told them, "Y'all go home and let nature take its course." He looked at his wife and said, "Come on, girl," and they went home.

Now, I want you to see that we prayed one time together—but their faith rose up. Something cracked inside their minds and they understood. Nine months later, a beautiful little baby girl was born to them. It was happiness at its best. That couple loved that baby, it was wonderful!

Eleven months after that...another baby was born. Well, they weren't quite as happy. Not that they weren't happy, they were just surprised and a little worn out. Well, fourteen months after that, another baby came! At that point, my friends came to our house.

"We got a problem here," the husband said, "Do you think we can pray and ask God to close her womb?" I thought it was funny.

I said, "You don't want to have any more babies?"

He just said one word, "No."

I said, "Quit sowing!"

The wife looked at me and said, "He can't do that! He loves me, he can't help himself. I love babies, Brother Jesse, I want a bunch of 'em!"

I looked at Cathy and her eyes lit up. I said to my wife, "Don't get any ideas, woman. One's enough."

My friend looked at me and actually said, "I just can't understand how that woman got pregnant."

I still laugh when I think about this situation. It shows you that God can do anything you can believe for—not fear-based begging, but real faith that is peaceful, calm, hopeful and ready to receive.

Just be careful when you're like that...or you might end up like this couple with more, way more, than you imagined.

## You Can't Fit Christ into Your Philosophy

You can't fit Christ into your preconceived philosophies. You must be led by what He says, not by what you want.

If you take Christ and try and fit him into your doctrines, He won't fit. The pure Word of God is endlessly powerful. You can't cram it into a religious idea. It doesn't fit. Of course, that doesn't stop people from trying.

A lot of Christians want to do what they want to do, regardless of what God's Word says. So they ignore some teachings in the Bible. They aren't ignorant. They just choose to alter the Word in order to keep some things they should get rid of.

In the Old Testament, people did a lot of things trying to fit Jehovah into their preconceived philosophies. When God sent His Son, it was not only to save the world, but to shine light on the truth about God's nature and the way life works.

The New Testament gave us a new covenant through Christ. It cut out all the little ways people could weasel and do what they wanted to do—living however they wanted to, then killing some goat or lamb as a covering for their sin and throwing it out in the desert.

No, once God sent Christ, greater accountability came. One sacrifice for all, pure and true enough for every generation past and present—giving us the ability to know the "unknown God" and live a higher style of life, one that is accountable for what we do, what we think, what we say and even what God says.

The truth of the Word *matters*. It's pure and powerful and it can't be made to fit into the vain deceit of some distorted doctrine. God will not animate deceit. He will not bring life to a lie. And, if we want to succeed with Him, we must avoid trying to fit him into our preconceived ideas. We must simply be led by what He says. That's why it's called *childlike* faith.

# CHAPTER 11

# *You Don't Have to Like Everything In the Bible*

There are some things in the Bible that I don't particularly like—and that's OK. God never told us we had to like everything, but He did encourage us to do what He said because it's the best way to live. Notice I said best, not easiest. I've found a lot of verses in that book that I just want to rip out! I'm not going to lie about it. Here are a few that come to mind...

*"Vengeance is mine, sayeth the Lord."* NO! Let it be mine. You take too long, God!"

*"Love your neighbor..."* You know you feel the same way about this one...you may not even *like* your neighbor!

*"...Bless those that curse you."* Have you ever been cursed out and thought, "I'm going to bless that guy with $20! I'm going to put it in his hand just as soon as he stops giving me sign language!"

*"Pray for those that despitefully use you..."* Has anybody ever ripped you off on purpose? Imagine one day, your husband comes

running in and says, "Honey, our friends just ripped us off! Isn't that wonderful? Let's pray for them!"

Even the disciples of Jesus wrestled with this one thinking, *How many times do I got to forgive this jerk of a brother I've got in a day?!* When Jesus told them seventy times seven, their brains tilted and all they could say was, "Lord, increase our faith!" (Luke 17:5). That's 490 times in a day! Can anybody stick you that much that you need to forgive that much? Don't answer that!

All of these kinds of verses smack up against our personal philosophy. They are some of the most dismissed verses in the Word, but they are still the Word. When we throw them out, we're not helping anybody...especially ourselves.

I've noticed that when I actually do these kinds of things, something breaks in me and helps me. There is power in going against the grain of your flesh. It is difficult emotionally, but once you get over that hurdle and simply agree to do it, God can step in and give you the grace to follow through. I find that the things that don't gratify my flesh are in actuality the things that make my life better in the long run.

It is amazing how applying these pure and simple wisdoms can actually bring peace to your life—you'd think they wouldn't, but they do. In fact, I've personally seen how just going ahead and doing what God said deflates the actual problem and how many times it turns a bad situation completely around. Go ahead. Try doing the ones you usually avoid. See for yourself!

## Wrinkles and Cream

My wife, Cathy, gets mad about how I treat my face. She's always trying to get me to put creams and lotions on my face.

"Your skin is going to look like leather if you don't take care of it," she says.

I tell her, "I like leather!"

I know it's all getting loose. I don't care. I know the lines on my forehead make me look like a Star Trek Klingon but, hey, it doesn't make a difference to me...I earned these babies!

Now, I do go shopping with Cathy and it seems like we always end up at a counter where they sell lotions. My wife can get so greased up with that stuff that you can't even hug her. *Foom!* She'll go flying right out of my hands, just slip right out!

I don't understand why women always want to be oiled up. It does smell good, but I can't take being covered in grease.

You know, I usually take showers but, not long ago, I decided to take a hot bath in the tub. Well, I put my foot in there and *foom!* I was on my backside. That tub had gotten so oiled up, it almost killed me. She knew it was oiled up and didn't tell me!

What did I want to do after I nearly broke my backside? I wanted to accuse her of trying to kill me with all her lotions and potions. I wanted to raise all kinds of hell. But I didn't...I turned the other cheek so to speak! I figured I was doing it as unto the Lord! Thank you, Jesus, for your grace...and that's all I'm going to say about that!

# CHAPTER 12

# *Prayers of Doubt and the Choices that Kill*

It's not often that I go to hospitals to pray for people because I'm always traveling. I'm also not a pastor and hospital visitation is most often done by pastors and the pastoral staff. But, I do get a chance to go every once in a while and I'll tell you what…I'm blown away by the genetically altered statements that fly around.

It happens when people need desperate help. They're dying with cancer, they're in terrific pain and the church has someone on the pastoral staff down there to the hospital to pray. That's the person who usually meets me.

"Brother Jesse, we're believing by faith for the Lord to heal her and raise her up out of this sickness!" I think, *Praise God! I agree with you!* Then, they hardly take a breath before telling me something like, "Brother Jesse, we want you to pray for her and we believe the Lord will heal her…but she looks bad. I'll tell you, if God doesn't do something, it's *over.*"

I can't tell you how many times this happens. Before we even get into the hospital room, people are filled with doubt and yet, once inside, the tongues and the nice words start flying. One person usually has the best words, things that start with, "Oh, most glorious heavenly Father..." while someone else kicks into the Pentecostal stuff. They are giving it their best shot, but inside their hearts, they are filled with doubt.

I think that if a preacher can't stand in faith for real with someone, then he or she should leave. Why play the game? If that person does go home to be with the Lord, God is going to get the blame for not healing them when in actuality, it is just the doubt of some genetically altered preacher.

Never forget that in times like this, what we see should not dictate our thoughts. We must get rid of our preconceived ideas. We can't pray in faith and, in the same moment, appease our fleshly tendency to doubt. They can't co-exist. We must see doubt for what it is—a total hindrance to the end-result we want—and break through it.

Faith is the opposite of doubt and Romans 10:17 tells us how faith comes to us, *"So then faith cometh by hearing, and hearing by the Word of God."* So if we want to doubt less, then we need to fill our ears with the Word more because that's how faith comes to us. So then, when doubt tries to creep up, we must ask ourselves, "What did Jesus *say*?!!"

In other words, we can't focus on what's negative about the outward circumstances and expect anything to change. We MUST focus on the Word of God—pure and simple. The Word doesn't appease the flesh, it supercedes the flesh. There is *life* in the Word!

## No Spare Tires!

I know one preacher right now on television that's got thousands of members in his church—and although he is married, he has gotten two other women in his church pregnant. The whole church knows about it and doesn't seem to care.

Do you know what was said about it?

"Every man needs a spare tire."

How in the world can anyone believe such a thing? How could anyone ever go to a church whose leadership lives that way?

These are the guys who always talk about David and Bathsheba—they relate themselves to David and are proud about it! But, David is not supposed to be our example. JESUS is our example! David was an old covenant man and he paid a heavy price for that weakness. His children even dealt with it.

When things like this happen and people tolerate it, it smacks of genetically altered teaching. When the sexual mentality of the world dictates what happens in the church, it's a sad day for the people.

Don't think it was any better in "the good old days." There was a time in the Old Testament when some genetically altered person told everyone else it was OK to have "temple prostitutes" as long as the temple got some of the money. Now, whose mind got so low that it actually seemed like an OK idea to sell sex at church? Where do people get ideas like that? It's vain deceit and yet, totally against God's Word!

## They Sent Two Women to My Room!

Now, to show you the degree of vanity that goes on sometimes, I have to tell you this story. Once I agreed to speak at a church in Los

Angeles, California. It was run by a genetically altered pastor but I didn't know it at the time. I prayed and felt the Lord leading me to go. After all, it's really about the people, not the pastor anyway.

Well, I spoke that night and the service was just wonderful. The people were so hungry for God's Word, it was like feeding little birds that had been starved—they pulled on the spirit of God within me and I them gave everything I had. I left to go back to my hotel room.

Well, I was a little hungry so I ordered room service. It was about 10:30pm and they told me it'd be thirty minutes. Only fifteen minutes passed and I heard a knock at the door. I thought, *Man, I guess there aren't too many people ordering food tonight.*

I opened up the door and instead of a guy with a cart of food, there were two beautiful women.

"Hello, Brother Jesse. We work for the church," they said.

"Oh, great," I said, not thinking.

"We came here to minister to you," they said.

Now, stupid me, I didn't understand what they were saying. I said, "What? Minister to me?"

The looked at me more intently and said, "You know...we were told by the Pastor that anything you need, we're here to supply."

I still didn't get it because it was the furthest thing from my mind. After all, we'd just had a knock down, drag out, God-filled service. So, I looked around the room and said the only thing that came to mind.

"Well, my Lord, y'all already gave me a nice fruit basket. Everything's fine," I told them, smiling, trying to reassure them that I was fine.

One of the women looked at me and tried to give me a hit, "*Anything* else you need?"

"No," I said, "I don't need a thing."

"I'm serious," she replied, "we can be a blessing to you."

And, then, it hit me...it was like an alarm finally went off in my head. Ding! Ding! Ding!

I looked at them and said, "Are y'all saying what I *think* y'all are saying?"

They smiled and said, "Well, *yes*."

I couldn't believe it. I was so shocked.

I looked at them both and said, "Girls, go home. You've been deceived. You're temple prostitutes." I sent them away.

The pastor called me later on and he told me, "You're just old fashioned."

I told him, "No, I'm saved. I'm born again." There is verse that I always think of when I remember this situation. It's God telling us in 1 Peter 1:16, "...*Be ye holy; for I am holy.*"

I thought to myself, *This guy isn't going to last.* In fact, I told him when he dropped me off at the LAX airport, "You're not going to live long. You have prostituted the Gospel and you must be very good at what you do because you actually convinced two women that that was OK. I'm going to pray for your soul. I don't want you to go to hell but, in this situation, son, if you don't change, you going to hit that place."

Sure enough, it wasn't more than about eight months later that I heard he passed away. It was terrible. Did God kill him? No, but I believe *sin* did.

You see, you can get so genetically altered that you open the door for all sorts of trouble. It's not God or even the devil that is going to bring you down. You'll do it on your own. The wages of sin is death and, when you reject what you *know* is right, you are in a mentally and spiritually self-destructive mode—and your own body will turn on itself.

## Diluted With Human Opinions

The Word is pure—and the pure milk of the Word must not be mixed or diluted with human opinions. I love what 1 Peter 2:2-3 says, *"As newborn babes, desire the sincere milk of the Word, that ye may grow thereby: If so be ye have tasted that the Lord is gracious."*

That pastor diluted the sincere milk of the Word. He had distorted opinions that were diametrically opposed to the Word. He believed that women were mere objects to be used and that, as a man of God, he had the right to use as many as he wanted. That is not justified anywhere in the Word of God!

Instead of letting the Word transform his thinking, he diluted and dismissed what he read in the Word and became further conformed to the world. This is an "anything goes" and "whatever feels good is good" world but, that is not what God said is right—because it's not good for mankind to live this way. That's why God gave us His Word. To help us learn how to live well and not use and abuse each other. Love doesn't use and it doesn't prostitute anything.

If you're a Christian who is always looking for ways to appease your flesh instead of crucify your flesh, you're going to end up in a load of trouble. The flesh can't be satisfied. It always wants more and more. If you've got a weakness, don't look for scriptures to support it—that's diluting the Word with human opinion. Instead, look for scriptures to help you conquer it.

One of my favorite passages in the Bible is Galatians 2:20-21. I quote this to myself to conquer my flesh and build myself up—it inspires me! Read it aloud.

*"I am crucified with Christ: nevertheless I live; yet not I, but Christ liveth in me: and the life which I now live in the flesh I live by the faith of the Son of God, who loved me, and gave Himself for me.*

*"I do not frustrate the grace of God: for if righteousness come by the law, then Christ is dead in vain."*

## You Can't Satisfy the Flesh, It Always Wants MORE

Before I was saved, I was a good sinner. I did things that men dreamed of doing. I was in the rock world—so it was about booze, drugs, and women…hundreds of women. But, after I got born again, I dropped all of that and went full force towards Jesus.

I can honestly say that I have had more fun as a believer than before when I lived that old life because it's all real and clear now… and I actually remember what I did the next day!

I'm not carrying around all that baggage that kept pushing me towards getting as much earthly pleasure as possible so that I could fill up that void. That sin that clung to my heart was always pushing me to find more drugs, more booze, more women…it was never enough, because it didn't meet the real need.

Redemption met the real need. So, when you're a Christian and you find your flesh trying to push you to dilute the Word in order to appease itself, you need to go to God and fill up with Him. No matter how much you try, your flesh is never going to be satisfied.

The drug you swallow or shoot in your veins is never going to be enough. The drinks you get drunk on one day won't bring satisfaction the next. You'll want more. Food can't fill the hunger for real peace, love, or joy. The immorality you engage in will just bring you to the point of wanting to do more and more.

You see, trying to make yourself feel good by external means when you are lacking internally never works. It's temporary. When it comes to the flesh, the want always grows more and more and the satisfaction gets less and less—because whatever it is that your flesh *thinks* can satisfy doesn't have the *power* to satisfy.

You can't satisfy a spiritual need with something physical or sexual. No matter how much you do, that fact won't change. You can spend your whole life trying, but only Christ the hope of Glory living *in* you and *through* you can meet that deep need.

That's why you have to draw close to Christ every day. That's why sowing the Word of God into your mind and heart is so important. If you don't have daily fellowship with Jesus and have His Word part of your everyday life, your flesh *will* try to substitute. It will try and fill your spiritual need with something physical…and it will make that substitute look more alluring than you ever dreamed it could look. Never forget that!

# CHAPTER 13

## *Be Open to Learning From Everyone*

Before God blessed me with an aircraft to fly all over the world, I either flew commercial or drove to my meetings. I loved the meetings I could drive to because I loved driving—I still do. I enjoyed that quiet time on the road.

I can drive all night and I don't get tired until the sun comes up, for some reason. I guess it's because I've worked at night for so long. You know, entertainers and rock musicians usually work nights. Preachers speak at night a lot too.

The aircraft helps me to do a lot more. I probably speak five times more than I did before God blessed me with it which means I'm reaching more people for Jesus. But the only thing I don't like about it is that I can't do the things I used to do. In the early years of my ministry, when I drove a lot, I enjoyed stopping at different churches as I drove home.

Sometimes I'd drive 14 hours to get home, driving both at night and in the day, and as I'd pass by a Baptist church, I'd think, "I sure could use a good Baptist sermon...I just need to hear some salvation!" Those Baptists know how to preach on salvation. I want to answer every altar call they give! I almost forget I don't need it; they make it sound so wonderful.

Sometimes I'd drive by a Methodist church and stop for their service so I could hear something about the grace and mercy of God. They're masters at sharing God's Word on that subject. I can remember leaving their services and thinking, *Man, I'm going to be more merciful, I'm going to be more of a blessing.*

Then, sometimes, I'd just say to myself, "I need some fire, man! I need something hot! I'm talking kicking, Pentecostal-Tabasco sauce style church! " So, I'd stop in at one of those little Pentecostal churches and I could hear the screaming and hollering before I even opened the door. Those places are on fire!

I especially loved stopping in at the black Pentecostal churches. I'd listen to them holler and sing and wave handkerchiefs in the air. The people are great but nobody preaches like a black Pentecostal preacher—they don't just holler, they hoop! It's like listening to a song, the rhythm is great. Those preachers have got more breath-power and extra syllables going on than anybody I've ever heard...and I'm Cajun, so we say all kinds of things people have never heard of.

Man, preachers would get the church so fired up that the people would stand up on top of the pews and shout back at the preacher to keep going. It was wonderful! I'd go to one of those knock-down, drag-out services and think, "These people have got power!" I'd walk out charged up, wishing I was black.

You know, even if everything you hear isn't right, you can still enjoy the service—using the wisdom God gave you to absorb what is good and profitable to your spirit and throw out the genetically altered parts. Being teachable and learning to find the good in what you hear is vitally important. Every denomination has something they do well.

## "I Know That Already, Brother Jesse!"

The only churches I don't enjoy are the ones that refuse to accept the good in other churches' teachings. Its as if they think their way is the only way and they won't even accept the good in those outside their "camp" so to speak. The Word of God is rich and varied. It's transforms people from the inside out who apply it with the right heart. And there are many wonderful teachings out there.

If you're hearing it but it's not doing anything for you then, you're either not really *hearing* it or you're not applying it. That's why God told us to meditate on His Word day and night. It has to get in us in order for us to be able to pull on it and apply it to our lives.

God's Word is more than a self-help book. It's not about you doing all the principles just right—no, it requires you to recognize God in you and let His presence live through you, so that you are transformed from the *inside* out.

So, when I hear someone say, "I know that already" but their life is either lethargic or a mess, I realize they may know it but they don't *know* it! You see, when you *know* something, it changes you.

In 2 Timothy 1:12 (NKJV), the Apostle Paul said, *"For this reason I also suffer these things; nevertheless I am not ashamed, for* **I know Whom I have believed** *and am persuaded that He is able to keep what I have committed to Him until that Day."*

Paul went beyond being a believer—he became a knower. *Whew!* When that happens to you, things change because suddenly, you start walking in faith. There is no lazy, "I know it already" attitude in that zone. It is the opposite. It is a hunger for more of God attitude—hunger for more freedom, more life, more of all the good things God has to give.

In that frame of mind, you are moving in the same realm as Abraham—believing for something high! He was aiming to be a father of many nations, a promise God had given him, even though his wife was old and barren. That's not lazy thinking!

The Word says, *"He **staggered not** at the promise of God through unbelief; but was **strong** in faith, giving glory to God; And **being fully persuaded** that, what He had promised, He **was able** also to perform. And therefore it was imputed to Him for righteousness"* (Romans 4:20-22).

Notice that God rewarded his faith with *righteousness*. That's how important that *knowing* and *fully persuaded* thinking is to God.

Listen, when you think you know it all, you are genetically altered! Nobody knows it all but God! There is always something to learn and explore in the Word of God and God's people. Just avoid the genetically altered views by looking for the spark of real faith— the teaching that pushes you to think higher and believe better about God and His will for you.

Remember, the spirit is always higher than the flesh, so the teaching should push you higher towards God...where you belong.

# CHAPTER 14

# Who Knows the Mind of the Lord?

We think of the word "anti-Christ" as only to be used for the end-times, but the truth is that "anti" simply means against. So, anything that is alters the truth of Christ is a teaching that is *"anti-Christ"* in that it misses the motive and the message.

God gave us His Word knowing that it would take His Spirit to truly grasp it. That's why His Word reiterates that we should live our lives "in Christ" or "in Him."

*"For in Him,"* or in Christ, *"dwelleth all the fullness of the godhead bodily"* (Colossians 2:9). That is a powerful scripture. Imagine it! All God is, is found in Christ. When you accept Jesus, your spirit is re-created to house His Spirit…which means that you have amazing potential.

## The Anointing to Know All Things

1 John 2:20 says, *"But ye have an unction from the Holy One, and ye know all things."* "Unction" means a smearing of the anointing. In other words, when He is "on you" you can "know all things."

So, that's why the Word instructs us in Romans 12:2, *"And be not conformed to this world: but be ye transformed by the renewing of your mind, that ye may prove what is that good, and acceptable, and perfect, will of God."* After all, how can you know His will—His way of thinking and being—unless you "renew" or allow His Word to "transform" your mental state to the way He thinks?

Do you think it's possible to have a mind like Jesus Christ? It is! 1 Corinthians 2:16 asked the question and answered it in the same verse, *"For who hath known the mind of the Lord, that he may instruct him? But we have the mind of Christ."*

So, you—yes, YOU—have the *same* potential the disciples had after they accepted Christ's sacrifice on the cross and received His Holy Spirit into their hearts in the Upper Room. What potential? To understand the *"mind of Christ"* which housed the *"fullness of the God-head bodily."* We're talking about God's mind here! Imagine it!

Imagine knowing how He thinks, having what inspired the Word inside *your* mind?! As you renew your mind which will equip you with faith, you will be able to grasp the life-changing truth of His Word—first at a spiritual level and then, at a mental level too. The anointing of God is on His Word and when you sincerely seek Him through it, it will come on you and open your mind to its truth, so that *your* mind begins to understand the mind of Christ and literally supercedes natural thought. Glory!!

WHO KNOWS THE MIND OF THE LORD?

## Recognizing "AntiChrist" Words and Ways

When that happens, you will get to a place where you immediately notice "antiChrist" statements—teachings and words and attitudes that are diametrically opposed to the mind of Christ.

It doesn't happen overnight because your mind needs practice with the things of God, but as you grow and mature and keep a pure heart towards God, that purity will push out the pollution of the world that has been programmed into your brain and it will turn your thought process back to what is right. God's ways are right ways, plain and simple.

It is the mind of Christ—which houses who God is—that will lead you to break free from natural thinking and go higher in your ideas about what you can do. You will get to the point of being able to say with confidence what St. Paul said in Philippians 4:13, *"I can do all things through Christ which strengtheneth me."* He wrote that in prison!

## Content—During the Heat

Paul the Apostle knew how to both live high and live low and he was content either way, because He *knew* Who was inside of Him. He knew that Christ would be there through thick and thin if he remained "in Christ." He knew that having God's Spirit both *in* him and *on* him would take him to a higher place in life.

Paul was able to withstand pressure and persecution because of that. He could be content even in the heat of being attacked, spoken evil of and thrown in prison. Not because he was some big, strong man but because the Christ inside of him had taken precedence—he *knew* in Whom he *believed.*

2 Timothy 1:12 says it best when it says, *"For the which cause I also suffer these things: nevertheless I am not ashamed: for I know Whom I have believed, and am persuaded that He is able to keep that which I have committed unto Him against that day."*

The next verse he tells us how to do that too. *"Hold fast the form of sound words, which thou hast heard of me, in faith and love which is in Christ Jesus."* You see, it's the "sound" words of God that you hold onto in faith and in love that help you through anything.

Being in Christ is how Paul was able to think higher and gain revelations that would come to rock the known world. Paul knew that, no matter what, the spirit in him would guide him, reveal things to him, and that God would make a way of escape when the timing was right.

## You Can Be Complete

After you read Colossians 2:9, *"For in Him dwelleth all the fullness of the Godhead bodily"* then, you can better understand verse 10 which says, *"And ye are complete in Him, which is the head of all principality and power."*

Complete is a powerful word. It comes from a Greek word that means to *cram full* like a net full of fish or to *level up* like filling a whole with dirt—and also to *furnish, satisfy, execute, finish,* and *verify.*

If something or someone inside of you could do all that for you, in any situation in life, you'd say that you'd be complete, right? Well, guess what? You DO have that Someone inside of you, if you are born-again, and that means you have the potential to be the kind of person and live the kind of life God intended.

## Principalities Work Through Personalities

Notice also that the Christ inside of you is *"the head of all principality and power."* In other words, no matter what power comes against you, the Power inside of you is above that in rank. **What's inside of you outranks whatever force is pushing against you from the outside.**

Sometimes we think people are our problem, but the truth is that it's the "antiChrist" force influencing those people that is our real problem. So, *principalities* work through *personalities.* Have you ever heard someone say, "That sister so and so is a devil from hell!" You might look at everything she is doing and believe it. Don't! It's not the woman; it's the principality or power influencing the woman.

That's why the Bible tells us that we shouldn't spend our lives wrestling with people—but instead fight the *principality* or *power* motivating them to say what they say and act the way they do. Ephesians 6:12 says, *"For we wrestle not against flesh and blood, but against principalities, against powers, against the rulers of the darkness of this world, against spiritual wickedness in high places."*

Again, the Christ in you is *"head of ALL principalities and powers"* which is why the next verse tells you to make sure your equipped with His protection. *"Wherefore take unto you the whole armor of God, that ye may be able to withstand in the evil day, and having done all, to stand"* (Ephesians 6:13). You can't do it on your own. You need to be in Christ.

So, what do you do when somebody is attacking you? You attack the *spirit* that is motivating them. You don't even need to be near them to do it. You can bind that spirit and pray against it, no matter where you are and no matter where they are. God's Spirit is not bound by time and place.

Just make sure that before you do, you're clean with God—ask forgiveness for whatever you've done, let the blood of Jesus wash away whatever is clinging to your soul.

Check yourself to make sure you are properly prepared with the whole armor of God so that you'll be able to withstand the heat. The Word gives you the full picture of God's armor and it will give you a good idea about God's protection: *"...Stand therefore, having girded your waist with truth, having put on the breastplate of righteousness, and having shod your feet with the preparation of the gospel of peace; above all, taking the shield of faith with which you will be able to quench all the fiery darts of the wicked one. and take the helmet of salvation, and the sword of the Spirit, which is the word of God; praying always with all prayer and supplication in the Spirit, being watchful to this end with all perseverance and supplication for all the saints"* (Ephesians 6:14-18).

Go to God in prayer and ask Him to show you if you're weak in one area of that armor—knowing that it's not you that creates or fashions the armor. It is God's armor. You can only be suited up in it by dwelling in Him—obedience is better than sacrifice.

Remember that, as a believer, everything you do to shore yourself up is only for your own good. Life will hit you from many sides. But, for those who know who they are in Christ—in whom they have *believed*—there is greater strength. It's not just something to pull on when you need it, but Someone to pull on during the heat of life.

Every step you take towards allowing Christ to live through you is a step towards your good future. You don't have to rely on your own thoughts and your own strength. God knows all. In Him is the fullness of the Godhead body and He lives inside of you. As you equip yourself with more of Him, you will be ready for all things.

*"For who hath known the mind of the Lord, that he may instruct Him? But **we** have the mind of Christ."*

1 Corinthians 2:16

# CHAPTER 15

# *The Truth About "God Is In Control"*

Traditions says the Lord owns it all, but does He? Sure, God created this world—and while He does technically have ownership rights, most people who use this statement do it in what I call a genetically altered way. They pretend as if He is solely in contol and that they are powerless and at the mercy of life. That is not how God set it up to be! We have been given authority. We have been given power.

Just look at what Genesis 1:27-28 says, *"So God created man in His own image; in the image of God He created him; male and female He created them. Then God blessed them, and God said to them, 'Be fruitful and multiply; fill the earth and subdue it; have dominion over the fish of the sea, over the birds of the air, and over every living thing that moves on the earth.'"*

So who gets the benefit if we run this planet well? We do and everything that swims, flies, creeps and moves on it. And, who gets destroyed if we don't take dominion and rule properly? We do and again, everything else that lives and moves on the planet.

*Again, "Beware lest any man spoil you through philosophy and vain deceit, after **the tradition of men**, after the rudiments of the world, and not after Christ"*

Colossians 2:8

The traditions of men are powerful. In fact, if you read Mark 7:13, Jesus says, *"Making the word of God of none effect through your tradition, which ye have delivered: and many such like things do ye."*

So, adhering to church tradition—without wisdom, real faith, or the right motive—has the capability to make God's Word *ineffective*. Think about that! Do you realize what that's saying? It is saying that a man-made tradition has the ability to make the Word of God useless….and I know that I'm kicking a sacred cow over when I say this, but it must be said.

**The only way the "traditions of men"**
**can have the power to make God's Word "of none effect"**
**is if God is NOT in control.**

Now, don't let that shock you! Centuries and centuries of church teaching have continually reminded us that God is *always* in control…but that is not true. It sounds true, but it is *not*. Stick with me here! So, how can that be? It is possible because God, in His infinite wisdom, *chose* to give us free will ownership over this planet. Here is the scripture that proves it:

*"The heaven, even the heavens, are the LORD's: but the earth hath He given to the children of men."*

Psalm 115:16

God is not in control on this planet, because He gave it to us. If He was still in control, we'd have no rape, no murder, and no malice. If you want to go where God is in control, go to Heaven. There is no poverty, sickness, misery, recession, depression in Heaven—none of that! Nobody is talking bad about somebody else. Nobody is trying to hurt others. Why? Because in Heaven, God is in control.

When does God regain control? When He comes back during the millennial kingdom—when the scripture tells us that the lion will lay down with the lamb. In other words, peace! When God's in control, there isn't any killing and stealing.

Notice this: when *God* is in control, *Satan* is shut down. So, if you are waiting on God to do everything for you, you're going to wait a long, long time. He will fulfill His Word to you...but you must recognize that you are not a puppet on a string, you are not a piece in a puzzle...you have a measure of responsibility to take authority in the situations of your life.

## The Old Blame Game

You see, the traditions of men always end up blaming God. Because He is all-powerful they assume He will be all-controlling... but He is not. It is a predicament of free will. It is a predicament of being given such responsibility. Again...it bears repeating! *"The heaven, even the heavens, are the LORD's: **but the earth hath he given to the children of men"*** (Psalm 115:16 NKJV).

So, when something doesn't go right, who gets the blame? If we're talking about the traditions of men, God usually gets the blame. *He* gets blamed when we don't do *our* job! He gets accused over things He has given us the responsibility to do. Who is His chief accuser? Satan. He has a purpose in altering our viewpoints. He wants us to develop those "traditions of men" that will make the

Word have no "effect" in our lives. He is a liar and a thief, not only out to harm us but to discredit His adversary, God.

## Taking Ownership
### I Cannot Meet God's Needs

I've said it so many times...if you don't take *ownership* over what is yours, someone else will. Someone *will* control your environment if you let them. You can actually have a good heart and mean well, but if you are living without taking your God-given responsibilities, then you will not get God's best in life. How could anyone possibly receive His best if they don't do their part?

Some things are your job. Some things are God's. He has obligated himself to fulfill His Word—His condition is for *you* to have faith in Him and obey His Word. So, if you do your part, God will do His part. Like I mentioned earlier in this book, God can sovereignly do whatever He wants but He never goes outside of His own Word—He won't break His Word.

> *"My covenant will I not break, nor alter the thing that is gone out of my lips."*

Psalm 89:34

## This Ministry Is More Than I Can Handle

I've learned that God can and will do anything I can believe Him for, anything that I can follow through with all the way. Because of this, I don't feel overly pressured by the weight of what He has called me to do, build or accomplish...instead, I feel free knowing that if I do *my* part, He will do *His*.

This ministry God gave me is bigger than me. Without faith in God and obedience, I could not handle it. You see, I learned early on that I cannot do it alone. I'm not that good! If I let it, the pressures of just trying to keep the thing running and continuing to do good works would be more than I could stand.

I learned very early in my ministry that I cannot meet the needs of this ministry—financially especially. Television bills alone are money-eaters. The sheer numbers are staggering and would be overwhelming if I thought about handling it on my own.

Trying to reach people and change lives with His Word around the world is a huge endeavor…for *me*. You see, the most important thing I learned about releasing the pressure is this: *Every* need this ministry has is not *my* need…it is *God's* need.

I cannot meet *God's* need. Only He can do that. Knowing that brings me great relief. If I do my part, God will do His—and my part is not nearly as hard as His! His job is to open hearts to the message, to bring in the finances to fulfill the vision, and to equip me with what I need to do what He has called me to do—spiritually, physically, financially and in every other way.

My responsibility is to keep my heart and my head in line with Him. In other words, trusting Him and obeying Him, and letting Him guide me to the right decisions for His ministry. *That* I can do!

## Why I Can't Care

I had a man get really mad at me not long ago when I was talking about the financial responsibilities of the ministry. I guess it bothered him that I wasn't acting worried like he thought I should be, given the magnitude of responsibility.

He told me, "You don't seem to care about anything!"

I looked at him and said, "You're right, I couldn't care less."

This irritated him. He thought I was just being cocky. But the truth is that I've learned to throw off the cares of this world. It doesn't mean the devil doesn't attack me. It doesn't mean that my mind doesn't try to get caught up in the situation. It doesn't mean the devil doesn't try to weigh the cares of the ministry on my mind and on my shoulders.

What it means is that, at the end of the day, I've learned that the only way I can do what God has called me to do is to *cast* all my care upon Him...knowing that He cares for me. I must throw it off. I don't do it because I'm irresponsible. I do it because I am responsible. If I were to try and take on the pressure of it all, it would kill me and I would forfeit my calling by trying to do something I was never given the right to do. This passage makes it clear to me.

> *"Humble yourselves therefore under the mighty hand of God, that He may exalt you in due time:*
>
> *Casting all your care upon Him; for He careth for you.*
>
> *Be sober, be vigilant; because your adversary the devil, as a roaring lion, walketh about, seeking whom he may devour:*
>
> *Whom resist steadfast in the faith, knowing that the same afflictions are accomplished in your brethren that are in the world.*
>
> *But the God of all grace, Who hath called us unto His eternal glory by Christ Jesus, after that ye have suffered a while, make you perfect, stablish, strengthen, settle you.*
>
> *To Him be glory and dominion for ever and ever. Amen."*

> 1 Peter 5:6-11

## True Humility Ain't What You Think!

Do you know what true humility is? It's knowing that God is bigger than you are—and that what He says is true, regardless of what others say. It's recognizing that He has given you responsibility and *taking* it. It's recognizing that He has given you wisdom in His Word and *taking* it.

In other words, it's putting Him *first* and you *second*. And if He tells you that He's given you and your children the earth as a *gift*… then, it's receiving that gift and its responsibilities and running with it. It's being confident in your position.

Humility is oftentimes taking ownership over what belongs to you—it's not shucking responsibility and blaming God when things don't turn out the way you like.

So, humility is first. That's the only way you can fulfill the next verse, *"Casting all your care upon Him; for He careth for you."* You can't give God something unless you believe that He can be trusted…and you can't believe He can be trusted unless you bow your knee and recognize that He is *God*.

It's foolish to think He is incapable of dealing with your situation. He is GOD. Humble yourself under *"His mighty hand"* so that He can *"exalt you in due time."* He didn't inspire words like "His mighty hand" lightly. This tells us that God will work for us, but it isn't until "due time" that we see success. First, you sow. Then, you reap. It works in all facets of life. So, humility to God and His Word are the first steps to living without worry.

## "Care" Is a Form of Pride

Care is a form of pride. Worry is a form of pride. It's opposite of humility. When you choose to worry and take on the cares of this world, you are essentially saying that God can't handle it. That you've got to take it out of "His mighty hand" and worry about how to fix it yourself.

"Well, don't you *care*, Brother Jesse?" you might ask. Well, I am *concerned*. There is a difference. I'm concerned so I pray, have faith and obey. But I don't allow concern to become a "care" or a "worry." You see, there is nothing wrong with being concerned. You can be concerned about something but you shouldn't take the load of it—the pressure. That's why the scripture tells us that we should be "casting" our cares upon the Lord. It's a continual throwing off of care. You may have to do it daily or even hourly!

Cares come up all the time. Why did He warn us to cast them upon Him? Because only He can handle the pressure. How do you cast the care of something that is really heavy? By realizing that *"He careth for you."* A lot of this is about recognizing His great love.

1 John 4:18 says, *"There is no fear in love; but perfect love casteth out fear: because fear hath torment. He that feareth is not made perfect in love."* When you know you are loved, your fear dissipates.

The greatest worriers are those who do not realize that God cares for them. They live in fear that He doesn't, that He won't, and that He never will...and so they must try and go through everything in life on their own. The pressure of living like that is terrible. It closes up your chest and takes its toll on you. It's not how God created any of us to live.

We do our part—humbly through faith and obedience. Our faith literally makes us "whole" because it's what's required to get God to do His part. His part is the harder part! He fulfills His Word to us and intervenes in our lives when necessary.

I hope you are getting this! I know it bucks at the traditions of men, but if you can get this as a revelation, it's going to literally change the way you think and live. You will be more blessed than you've ever been because you'll learn to tap into real faith and literally draw out what you need in life.

I'm talking about a real understanding of the "give and take" that comes from knowing that God and you must work together—that your part is to live in real humility, take real responsibility for what belongs to you, and obey God's Word.

When you trust that He always and forever cares for you, you'll see fear go, peace come, and blessings you never noticed or imagined start flooding your life.

# CHAPTER 16

# The Traditions of Men

The traditions of men are the accumulation of human theories transmitted from age to age. They're not fact, they're *theories*.

A lot of our scientific data is based on theory alone. It is not based on fact. Theoretical physicists say we have black holes—we haven't seen them, but we know they're there. The theory that Albert Einstein came up in 1905 was E=mc2. At first, it was a theory. Now, we know it to be a fact but for years, we based everything on that theory until it could be proven. Energy equals matter times the speed of light squared—that the speed of light is always constant.

Some theories become fact but most do not. The traditions of men are the same way. Sometimes the traditions of men sound good or feel good, and so we think they're right. The truth is that if they make God's Word of "none effect" like Jesus said, then they are just a bunch of distorted theories. They have "genetically altered" the Word. Here are some genetically altered statements that have become "traditions of men" that make the Word of no effect.

## "Sometimes He Does... and Sometimes He Doesn't" WRONG! That's Genetically Altered!

Or, here's a genetically altered statement, **"You know how God is, sometimes He does and sometimes He doesn't."** That's a slap in the face to God! Its like saying God is unreliable. It's a genetically altered statement out of a genetically altered Bible.

This kind of thing comes flying out of someone's mouth when they try something in the Word and don't see the results they want. Naturally, God gets the blame. Man always blames God first and rarely looks at himself—his heart, his true thoughts, and his life actions. These kinds of people will tell you not to try for anything much with God. It didn't work for them and it won't work for you either, they reason.

You've got to beware of the dream killers! These are the people who you share what God told you to do and the first thing they do is go against it. Why would someone immediately go against what you want to do for God? I'll tell you why...because God didn't give it to them! They have no revelation. They only have fear of the unknown and disappointment of their past experiences.

*Your* future should not be dictated by *their* past. That's the traditions of men in effect and they will make the Word of God in your life of no effect if you let them. Instead remember that your life is a gift from God and you have a measure of responsibility—let your life be dictated by trust, obedience and the supernatural laws of God, and the revelation He has personally given *you* through His Word. Dream-killers are everywhere!

## *"You Must Speak In the Same Kind of Tongues"* *WRONG! That's Genetically Altered!*

The Holy Spirit of God affects different people different ways. When people get the Holy Spirit with the evidence of speaking in tongues, they sound different from one another.

When I was growing up, my family eventually ended up in Pentecostal churches that were really bound by the genetically altered idea that everybody's prayer language ought to sound similar. I mean, if you didn't sound like the woman next to you, you didn't have "it." It was crazy!

I remember when, for years, all I ever heard in church was "Uhhh-shhundi!" or "Seee-Ki! See-Ki!" It wasn't until Kenneth Hagin came upon the scene that I actually heard what sounded like an entirely different language. One man sounded like he was speaking Chinese at times and, hey, maybe he was! God has done that before! He has given men language skills they did not have in order to reach people for Him. In fact, that's what actually happened in the Upper Room at Pentecost—God supernaturally gave them the ability to witness for Him.

When I think about it, a lot of them sounded like an old Honda trying to start up! "Uhhh-shhundi! Uhhh-shhundi! Uhhh-shhundi!" Now, it's funny but it isn't funny. What used to really confuse me in church was when someone would stand up and give a message in tongues that felt like it lasted twenty minutes, and then some other person would get the interpretation...stand up and tell it in fewer than 10 seconds. It was something like, "Thus saith the Lord, God....He said He'll do it!"

I used to think to myself, *I don't think that was all God said!* I mean they would talk in tongues forever and then you'd have a short interpretation. Sometimes, it would go the other way. The message in tongues would come to the congregation quickly, but the interpretation would run on for twenty minutes. I'd think, "Did God really say *that* much?!"

Later I realized that it's the gift of "interpretation" and not the gift of "translation"—meaning it doesn't always have to line up time-wise! God does some strange things! It doesn't mean they are not "Him" but His does work through people…so you've got to give them some slack!

1 Corinthians 13:12 puts it this way, *"For now we see through a glass, darkly; but then face to face: now I know in part; but then shall I know even as also I am known."*

There are some things we may not fully understand until we get to Heaven and stand face-to-face with the Lord. Who knows? Maybe then, I'll get the full revelation on "Uhhhh-shundi!"

## *If They Want to Hurt Homosexuals…*
## *They're WRONG! That's Genetically Altered!*

Now, I do not believe homosexuality is right—though I must say that, personally, if it weren't in the Bible, I wouldn't care who a person sleeps with. If this issue were not discussed in the Bible, I would not discuss it either. Personally, I believe in freedom and I don't think it's my business who a person loves or what they do in the bedroom. But, this issue *is* in the Word. This issue is very plainly spoken against in the Word of God. So, if I'm asked, I always show love to people but I always side with God.

So, it really bothers me when I see the venom and bile that some Christians have towards people living in homosexuality. I see supposed Christians on television holding up signs and hurling insults or beating people up that they think aren't living right. The last time I saw Christians on the news standing with hate-filled signs at a gay man's funeral, it made me feel angry. Why would anyone want to bring further hurt to a family who has just lost their son, regardless of his lifestyle? And why would they want to do such a thing in the name of a loving God? It's terrible.

God never called us to attack others because of what they may or may not be doing right—and this includes homosexuality or any other sexual sin. It's not our job to bring hatred to the world but to show people the love of Jesus. God is the judge and believe me; He will handle His business when it comes to humanity. We will all stand before Him one day.

But, the old traditions of men have brought us to the place where many Christians actually believe that its OK to hate or harm homosexuals since what they are doing is spoken negatively of in the Word of God—but again God didn't call us to be their judge. He called us to speak the truth in *love*. He doesn't put a cap on His rule to "love others as yourself" when it comes to homosexuals. Whether you think what they are doing is the worst sin or not, you have no right to hate. The only person we are allowed to hate is the devil.

Does that mean you can never voice what the Word says about homosexuality? No, of course not. I see a lot of preachers who refuse to answer the question of what they believe when it comes up. Why? Because we live in society now that calls it intolerance when you disagree with the reigning societal norm. But, I'm not interested in placating. Now, I'm not interested in fighting either but I will say what I think.

The tricky part is that, today, you can be accused of "hate speech" simply by agreeing with the Bible—which is wrong but it is why so few preachers will preach out of Romans chapter one! They are afraid to be labeled a hater but, the truth is that, the Word does deem homosexuality to be unnatural and an abomination. So, you should have the freedom to express that is what you personally believe. But, here is the key, that freedom doesn't give you the right to speak with *hatred* and it especially does not give you the right to harm anyone over their sexuality. Who do you think you are?

When Christians act out of hate, they negate the message of Christianity—for God so *loved* the world that He *gave*. The message is about loving and giving. So, when Christians speak the truth in the Word about homosexuality, but they speak in hatred rather than in love, they make the motive of God's Word of no effect. His motive is to love and to give life.

Our faith must be mixed with love to work—in all areas. You see, we're not supposed to hurt people at any time, especially when they themselves are hurting. No, we are to let our light shine... period.

## If They Hate Black People Mixing with White People They're WRONG! That's Genetically Altered!

It's the same thing with interracial relationships. The traditions of men have always seemed to tell us that people of different color skins and cultures can't worship together...but this is genetically altered too. When we get to Heaven, there will be people of all colors and cultures so, if we are going to worship together there, what's the problem with worshiping together here?

A while back a pastor was talking to me about the music ministry at his church. He said, "Man, I'm having problems with my choir." I couldn't help myself. I told him, "It's because they're all white. You got to get some black people in there, man!"

You see, I don't have a problem pointing out the differences in cultures—it's the spirit in which you do it that matters the most. Do you point out differences with a heart that aims to cut or hurt? Then, you aren't walking in love.

---

But, to just ignore the differences as if they don't exist, well, that is just plain dumb. Each culture seems to have its strong points and the truth is, the black culture knows something about music. They seem to have natural rhythm and soul. They can move! They can out-dance most white people any day of the week. Plus, they've got some of the best singers I've ever heard in my life.

That's why I often say, "Forget your color, but never forget your culture." Color doesn't mean a thing. It doesn't matter what that skin looks like because if I cut any human being with a knife, each of us bleed red. I hate prejudice with a passion! God wants us to come together, not tear each other apart.

In Galatians 3:27-29, it says, *"For as many of you as have been baptized into Christ have put on Christ. There is neither Jew nor Greek, there is neither bond nor free, there is neither male nor female: for ye are all one in Christ Jesus. And if ye be Christ's, then are ye Abraham's seed, and heirs according to the promise."* In other words, none of that race stuff matters…the only difference is, are you *in Christ* or not? That's the only dividing line.

When I was a boy, people worried about getting a black man's blood if they needed blood at the hospital. They had different water fountains. They didn't let people mix in restaurants. It was that bad.

When I was younger, I used to wonder, "If a white man took a pint of a black man's blood, could he sing better?" That's crazy, isn't it?! When I first heard that old black country singer, Charlie Pride, I was just sure he got a transfusion with a white man's blood. Black people don't normally sing country and if they do, they don't usually sound like that! But, that guy sure did a good job on it. It had nothing to do with his color either. It had to do with his talent…which was opposite of his culture but it worked for him!

All of us are unique in some way, and some are more unique than others. We all have strengths and weaknesses in varying degrees and the culture we were raised in dictates a lot. But, we can't let the traditions of men stop us from being who we are, doing what we are meant to do, recognizing the good points in other cultures and not worrying about getting all mixed up together in worship towards the Lord. We were all literally created to be one body. And one vital key to living in peace, no matter what the other person is like, is to show respect.

# CHAPTER 17

## Stronger Than The Past

Before I was born again, I drank a fifth of whiskey a day. I might do other drugs and drink other drinks, but no matter what, my minimum intake was a fifth of either bourbon or scotch whiskey. That means I'd get up in the morning, eat some pancakes and drink a glass of bourbon. It began at breakfast. I also usually smoked a lid of dope a week on top of snorting cocaine. I liked pcp and crystal, etc. You name it, I did it. I took trips and never left my house.

When I got born again, on Labor Day weekend in 1974, it took me four months to get out of the music business because the people I was hooked up with were, well, they were of the "I'll make you an offer you can't refuse" persuasion. I had to finish out my contract. So, I sent Cathy back home to Louisiana with my daughter and I finished out my career as a rocker.

When I left, I didn't have a job to go home to but I knew God had told me to go home anyway. "How'd I know that?" Well, I heard His voice. I was a baby Christian and I knew just enough to be dangerous, but I did know that voice. Every baby knows Mama's voice.

When Mama talks, their little head will turn. Well, I knew God told me to go home, so I did.

I immediately began going to church and tried to volunteer. "Whatever y'all would like me to do, I'll do," I told them. They were a little nervous because I hadn't quite cut the hair the way I was supposed to cut the hair and to them that symbolized "the world." Today, my hair is white but back then, it was chocolate brown and down the middle of my back. It was the 1970s and I was a product of my generation.

The first thing they asked me about was my past. "Jesse, we've got to talk to you about your past..." they said and immediately wanted me to dredge up the details of my life of sin. Why do Christians do this? Because they are genetically altered! They do not believe what the Word says! They do not believe 2 Corinthians 5:17, *"Therefore if any man be in Christ, he is a new creature: old things are passed away; behold, all things are become new."* I was a new creature the moment Christ came into my life but for years, all church people wanted to do was dredge up my past and judge me by it.

## If They Say, "If You're Saved, Never Hang Around Sinners" They're WRONG! That's Genetically Altered!

This is one of the ways the Church got so incredibly insulated—by never leaving its own. But God didn't call us to just fill up the church. He called us all to be evangelists and bring people to the knowledge of His saving grace, which means He called us to increase the church.

He also gave us Jesus who regularly ate with sinners and shared not only His faith, but His time...and He is our highest example. So, why is it that the traditions of men are so intoxicating that we'd rather believe religiosity and hole up together of all the time instead of doing what God said? "Be ye fishers of men!" How can you catch fish if you don't throw the net where they are? Let the elevator go to the top!

So why do so many people believe that you should never hang around sinners once you get saved? One reason—the traditions of men—they assume you are so weak that you are going to fall into the sinful lifestyle, rather than you being so strong that you influence others to fall into yours! It's that simple. It's a genetically altered idea based on fear—fear that you will lose your faith…and that they will lose you out of their church.

Personally, I believe that is wrong. If Christ "the hope of Glory" is in me and that if "greater is He that's in me than he that's in the world" then I should be a lot stronger then any sinner who comes in front of me. I shouldn't have to stop talking to people or eating with people just because they don't know God like I do.

I can't tell you how many people have told me, "Brother, you can't ever get around booze because you used to drink so much… if you do, it'll grab you!" or "Man, if you were to get around drugs ever, you'd really be in trouble because you used to have such a problem with it. Be sure you never get around it because it'll get you!"

This sounds great and maybe it is advice for some people… people who haven't let Christ really come in and wash them clean. But, when I got saved, I got SAVED. The choice to choose Jesus changed EVERYTHING inside and therefore, my actions just followed suit.

You see, I didn't have a *problem* with drinking when I wasn't saved—no, I *enjoyed* drinking. It wasn't a problem to me; it was a lifestyle I was willing to ride all the way to the grave. I didn't have a problem with happy hour—I just believed it should last for ten hours. So, I didn't come to Jesus because I had a problem with booze or drugs. Those were just outward affects of a heart issue. My problem was that I didn't know God and didn't have the tools to crucify my flesh—but once I let Him tap into my heart, He helped me get exactly what I needed to let go of all that. What did I need? One thing, really. I needed HIM.

Again, *"Therefore if any man be in Christ, he is a new creature: old things are passed away; behold, all things are become new"* (2 Corinthians 5:17). I became something new.

So, when people told me that I could never get around booze again or I'd fall, I would think, "What? Haven't you read the Word? I'm changed!" They were genetically altering 2 Corinthians 5:17.

Over the years, I've quoted that verse to many people who warned me about booze and I've found that they all say about the same thing back: "Well, I know but..." There is always a *but* in the way. Even that is genetically altered! It is essentially saying, "I know God's Word says that but it isn't true...it's not *realistic.*" Yeah, they're right. It's not realistic. It is spiritual, not natural, and it is pure divine truth. God's ways always supersede natural thinking.

My words back are usually about the same, "Wait a minute, what is our foundation for living for Jesus? What power do we base our salvation upon?" In other words, the same *Jesus* who saved me is the One who changed me into a new creature.

I'm not saved by *tradition.* I'm not saved by good *sermons.* I'm not saved by *friends* who are well-meaning but stuck in some old genetically altered *religion* either. Why should I have to allow somebody *else's* weaknesses and past mistakes govern *my* future? **I'm saved by the blood of Jesus...and it is *more* than enough to keep me in all situations.**

Still, no matter what I say, I've had preachers tell me, "Well, many people came to Christ just like you did and they fell by the wayside when they got around alcohol and drugs."

My response? "That doesn't mean *I'M* going to do that!" In other words, I refuse to allow the traditions of other men to dictate what the blood of Jesus has done in my life. Besides, what should I do? Never eat in a restaurant because they serve whiskey? Never go to a party? Insulate myself until I'm as religious as a monk? Look, I could be in a Jack Daniel's whiskey factory and it wouldn't make a difference...Jesus has made me FREE!

*Therefore if the Son makes you free, you shall be free indeed.*

John 8:36

## Stronger Than The Past
### Women and the Lust

The other thing they warn me about is women. I was a rock musician in the 1970s and my lifestyle was bad. The truth is I can't tell you how many times my wife, Cathy, would be in the hotel and other women would knock on the hotel door and ask Cathy if they could go to bed with me.

Looking at me today, you might not believe it but that was the way it was in the 1960s and the 1970s rock scene. It's still like that today, probably worse. But, back then it was all free love and drugs—flesh to the hilt. Cathy would holler, "No!" and slam the door in their faces.

After I came to the Lord, I was shocked at how many preachers and Christian men I met who wanted to dredge up my past exploits with women. They wanted to hear the stories. They enjoyed it.

I was also shocked at all the warnings I got from preachers that I had to "watch it" when it came to women and that because of my past, I was "just heading for adultery"—as if my past sin was going to dictate my future morality. I couldn't believe that they assumed I was the same old sinner. I couldn't believe that they didn't understand what getting saved had done for me—that they had so little understanding of the power of the blood of Jesus. They were completely genetically altered warnings.

How in the world am I going to insulate myself from women? Females make up more than 50% of the population! They are running the world! And besides, I didn't ever really have a problem with *women*—I had a spiritual problem in that, I didn't know Jesus and consequently, I had a problem with feeding my flesh 24/7 and letting myself run wild.

Before I was saved, I sowed to the flesh, not the spirit, because that was all I had. It was all I thought could make me happy. I lived to please myself and I didn't care about anybody else because my world revolved around myself. That selfishness was birthed out of a heart that did not know Jesus or understand the ways of God—and because I did not know or understand Him, I didn't have His Spirit living within me to guide me.

You see, I didn't know that I was sowing to the flesh and would reap only destruction. Unlike some people who naturally stay within guidelines, I had no fear of the repercussions of my actions. I didn't practice self-control because I had no reason to. Because I had no God, I didn't read or apply His Word and so, I didn't have the spiritual tools to "crucify my flesh."

I was a natural man. 1 Corinthians 2:14 says, *"But the natural man receiveth not the things of the Spirit of God: for they are foolishness unto him: neither can he know them, because they are spiritually discerned."*

You see, before I was saved, my body ruled. After, Christ in me ruled. I got a new recreated spirit—again, I was a new creature. Now I had the tools necessary to combat the flesh. But, it was still my responsibility to actually do it. How? By letting the Spirit within me rule—to rely on Him, turn to Him, stop warring with my own flesh and just simply cast down whatever thought tries to get bigger or higher than my knowledge of Him.

*"For though we walk in the flesh, we do not war after the flesh:*

*"(For the weapons of our warfare are not carnal, but mighty through God to the pulling down of strong holds;)*

*"Casting down imaginations, and every high thing that exalteth itself against the knowledge of God, and bringing into captivity every thought to the obedience of Christ."*

2 Corinthians 10:3-5

Too many people just simply don't do this—they don't bring thoughts into captivity or remember who they are in Christ. Instead, they hide those thoughts and in doing so, further inflate their own flesh. Most only crucify their flesh on Sunday before they go to church but they let their mind run wild the rest of the week. That's a recipe for disaster.

Jesus Himself warned us in Matthew 26:41 that the flesh is a weak thing: *"Watch and pray, that ye enter not into temptation: the spirit indeed is willing, but the flesh is weak."* Notice, if you watch and pray, you won't even enter temptation. Because your spirit is WILLING to do the right thing all the time, not just some of the time.

So, why do you have to "watch"? Because if you don't, you just might be "deceived" into giving into your flesh.

*"Do not be deceived, God is not mocked; for whatever a man sows, that he will also reap.*

*"For he who sows to his flesh will of the flesh reap corruption, but he who sows to the Spirit will of the Spirit reap everlasting life."*

Galatians 6:7-9

I remember a time when I was first saved where they literally didn't allow the men to hug the women in church—that's genetically altered Christianity. If you can't hug another woman without lust coming out of you, something's wrong. Those old traditions have made the Word of God of none effect.

A genetically altered man will think that his flesh always has to rule when it comes to sex and lust—but that is not true. The same blood that "saved" you gives you the power to "keep" yourself out of trouble when it comes to the lusts of the flesh. 1 John 5:18 says, *"We know that whosoever is born of God sinneth not; but he that is begotten of God **keepeth** himself, and that wicked one toucheth him not."*

Notice, *you* do the "keeping" but it is the Spirit of God within you that gives you the ability to sin not. *You* do the casting down of imaginations. *You* do what Romans 12:2 says, *"And be not conformed to this world: but be ye transformed by the renewing of your mind, that ye may prove what is that good, and acceptable, and perfect, will of God."* So, you are the one in charge, but God gives you the tools to overcome all.

It's you who will put your spirit in line ahead of your body. If you sow to the spirit, you'll reap a good life and you won't be bound by lust. If you sow to the flesh, you'll inflate the flesh and reap corruption.

---

Refuse to be genetically altered! You have everything in you to be around sin and still "sin not." I don't care if it used to be your greatest temptation and sin before you came to know the Lord—the *Greater* One now lives in *you.*

## *Tell Your Feelings How to Feel, Don't Let Your Feelings Dictate What You Believe*

Some times, I don't want to preach. Sometimes, I'm just plain tired and I don't want to go to the church I booked. That may come as a surprise to some people, but it's the truth—I'm normal and human, and feelings like this come up.

I can't tell you how many times I've stood in front of a congregation dog tired and thought, "Oh, who cares? Let 'em all go to hell, Jesus, let's get out of here." I know, it's terrible but you know me—I'm an honest man and I'm just going to tell you what's going on in my mind. Now, do I do it? Do I cancel because I'm tired? NO! Do I just leave the pulpit when I feel like that? NO!

What do I do in those situations when my mind and my feelings want to rule? I literally say to myself, "Shut up feelings. You don't tell me how to *feel*, I tell you how to *believe*." Do you understand what I'm saying? Feelings change. They sway like the wind. Plus, when you are tired or not feeling well, your feelings get even stronger towards the negative and they want to dictate even more of your choices.

The wise person notices that and instead of getting trapped in the temporary emotion, they instead take what God said they could have and *"calleth those things that be not as though they were"* until they are. For instance, they may feel "weak" but will choose to obey the Word and "say" that they are "strong" (Joel 3:10). That's what you call *belief* overriding *feelings*, instead of the other way around.

Beliefs should *not* be swayed by the temporary nature of emotion. Why? Because feelings can't be trusted! If you get into the habit of following your feelings, instead of what you know God said, you'll never achieve the success God wants for you—spiritually, physically, financially, relationally, or in any other way. You will become the kind of person who the scripture calls "double minded" and "unstable in all his ways" (James 1:8). Notice it says ALL his ways. That means, double-mindedness affects *every* facet of your life.

What did God say? Well, if we're talking about sickness, the Word says He *"...will take sickness from the midst of thee"* (Exodus 23:25). It's a blessing on your life when you are righteous. And how do you become righteous? By accepting the blood sacrifice of Jesus Christ and accepting salvation. Because it was Jesus *"...Who his own self bare our sins in his own body on the tree, that we, being dead to sins, should live unto righteousness: by whose stripes ye were healed"* (1 Peter 2:24).

So, when Satan tries to attack my body, I remind myself of what God said and I say, "Excuse me, devil, God will take this sickness away, so I'm not accepting it as mine! And Jesus bore my sickness when He hung on the cross, so I'm not accepting it as a fact of life! NO!"

I answer the problem with the Word, yet my feelings are going haywire sometimes. I think, "Boy, this doesn't feel good, it doesn't feel good!" But, I put down the feelings and exchange them for the Word. I don't denying what's happening, I just choose to deny the emotion attached to wreck my faith in God. I choose to resist and even, attack, with my faith in God's Word.

You must not let your feelings tell you how you feel or tell you how to believe. Sometimes, people pray for healing and then say, "Well, I don't feel it." That doesn't have anything to do with it.

*You* are not a feeling! You are more than that—you are a person, and a recreated one through the power of the blood of Jesus. So, whatever you're feeling shouldn't be the motivating factor or the basis of your trust in God. You have God inside of you now! You don't have to be swung around by your emotions. You can instead, lean on your faith, what you know God has said in His Word.

You can stop, right where you, feeling the same way you feel, and turn it around with the Word. Pray for God to give you strength if your emotions are raging and He will do it!

When I feel strong emotions, I pray in the Holy Spirit. That helps to clean out the junk so that I can speak the Word with a clear heart. Then, I speak the Word over myself. I say what God said until His Word coming out of my heart and mouth *changes* my feeling—because *all* feelings change eventually. Why not speed up the process with the positive, life-changing, nature of the Word of God? It's called confession and I don't care what anybody says, if it is done with a pure motive and heart towards God, it works!

So, tell your feelings how to feel! Stop letting your feelings tell you how to believe! What did *God* say? Say that instead and you will see change in your life—change that begins in your heart, moves to your mind, and makes it way out in your actions which, in turn, bring amazing changes into your life.

# CHAPTER 18

# The Source and the Substance

There's nothing wrong with philosophy but Christ must be the source, substance, and standard for all religious philosophy—otherwise, it's not going to measure up. Colossians 2:9 says, *"For in Him dwelleth all the fullness of the Godhead bodily."* So, in other words, within Christ is all that God *is*. This means that when you base your philosophy purely on Jesus Christ, you are basing your philosophy not on opinion but truth.

## Recognize the Divine Intent of "NOW"

"Now" is a word that reflects time. When we look at Hebrews 11:1, we see that our faith is supposed to be continually in the present, *"Now faith is the substance of things hoped for, the evidence of things not seen."*

If you don't believe in that word 'Now' as it pertains to faith, you will drag out God's will for your life for years—because faith is what is needed to get anything God's way. The next verse tells us it is how those who went before you obtained a good report from God. Hebrews 11:2, *"For by it the elders obtained a good report."*

That chapter also tells us that we can't even please God without faith—and if we can't please Him, how can we expect Him to reward us? Hebrews 11:6 says, *"But without faith it is impossible to please Him: for he that cometh to God must believe that He is, and that He is a rewarder of them that diligently seek Him."*

Time is always involved. *"Now faith is..."* is what God's Word says, but the traditions of men turn it around and exchange God's statement for the question, "Is faith now?" They reverse it. They genetically alter it.

When do you want to feel joy? When do you want to have peace of mind? When do you want to feel safe? When do you want to be blessed? When would you like to receive healing? When do you want to see change? Those are the human questions. God's divine answer is, *"NOW faith is..."* It's the answer to a lot of our questions...but one we don't really always want to hear, because it requires something of us.

I find most Christians want God to drop everything on their heads out of Heaven. But God rarely works that way. If you look in the Word, you'll see He always requires faith and love. They are the foundational requirement for God and His Word to work on our behalf. They are the bare minimum and they are more than enough.

Mustard seeds and mountains aren't two things that go together, but the divinity of God's statement *"Now faith is..."* pushes those two opposites together and turns the tables on the natural laws of this world. What is impossible becomes possible through the human ability to exercise faith. It changes something in the spiritual and mental arena of a person and it ripples out, sometimes forcefully, into natural world, changing circumstances and paving the way for all sorts of great and small miracles.

The traditions of men put things off to the future all the time with a "maybe one day" attitude that is at odds against God's challenge to make faith NOW.

## Ask Anything In My Name

Most people do not like being child-like in their prayers when they get older. They think it's foolish. Yet, Christ Himself told us that we must become as little children to enter the kingdom. Luke 18:17 says, *"Verily I say unto you, Whosoever shall not receive the kingdom of God as a little child shall in no wise enter therein."* In other words, we must come to Him in simple, open-hearted faith— because that is what children do.

As we get older, one way we learn to deal with disappointment is to not expect anything but that is not God's way. He wants us to make a concentrated effort to have faith like a child.

When Christ told us to "ask anything" in His name, He meant it. The traditions of men tell us to never be so bold as to ask anything in His name. They want us to only pray like we are shooting dice and end our throw with a quick, "If it be thy will." But Christ Himself encouraged us to be bolder.

*"Most assuredly, I say to you, he who believes in Me, the works that I do he will do also; and greater works than these he will do, because I go to My Father.*

*"And whatever you ask in My name, that I will do, that the Father may be glorified in the Son.*

*"If you ask anything in My name, I will do it.*

*"If you love Me, keep My commandments.*

John 14:12-15

Christ is not afraid of what you can ask for—but He does want your heart directed at doing His will. He urges us to question whether we love Him according to whether we are keeping His commandments. In other words, are we making an effort to do what He said? Not for the work's sake, but because we just simply love Him?

This is where we may go wrong on our requests. James 4:3 says, *"Ye ask, and receive not, because ye ask amiss, that ye may consume it upon your lusts."* Motives of the heart mean something to Christ.

If you are concerned about God's will, go and look at Genesis chapter one and two and the last two chapters in the book of Revelation. Read them. It's just four chapters. *That's* the will of God for man, one hundred percent. Between Genesis one, two and the last two chapters in the book of Revelation are eleven hundred and eighty-six chapters of killing, stealing, and destroying by an arch enemy called Satan. Notice that those first two and last two greatly differ.

I believe in the second coming of Christ. When Jesus comes back, I believe that He is going back to Genesis one, two and the last two chapters in the book of Revelation. We start over. Man is going to walk in the cool of the day with God again.

So, what has happened to the Church? We haven't focused on those four chapters. We've taken the others and tried to keep the fight on with Satan when, in reality, what Christ did on the cross defeated him long ago.

Our fight now is not with Satan but with keeping our own faith. 1 Timothy 6:12, *"Fight the good fight of faith, lay hold on eternal life, whereunto thou art also called, and hast professed a good profession before many witnesses."* Notice that faith is a "good fight"…there isn't anything good about fighting Satan.

So, why are so many fighting a defeated foe? Because the traditions of men have told us that is who we are still fighting. Forget that. Turn your attention to where it belongs—less on the devil and more on keeping up your own faith.

### The River of Life, Nothing Else Satisfies
### You Can't Outgrow Christ

No one can ever outgrow Christ. Once you've tasted the River of Life, nothing else will fully satisfy. It's hard for me to understand why anyone would deliberately go back to their old life after knowing Christ. You know, I've never really thought of backsliding. What would I go back to? What does that old life have to offer me that is better than what I've found in Christ? I've tasted the River of Life.

In my opinion, the Apostle Paul was the greatest intellectual mind ever drawn to the realm of Christianity and I love what he said to the Galatians when he saw them going backwards.

> *"O foolish Galatians, who hath bewitched you, that ye should not obey the truth, before whose eyes Jesus Christ hath been evidently set forth, and crucified among you?"*

Galatians 3:1

I'm Cajun, so we would say something more like, "You stupid fish head idiot! Whose spell are you under? Who got you to believe that?!"

It's foolish to turn away from Christ. Paul believed that someone had to have filled the Galatians' minds with vain philosophy for them to turn back as they did. He was so disappointed that they stopped obeying the truth. He was so disappointed that they had been "bewitched" into obeying something other than the Christ's truth.

You know, people who have known me since the beginning of my ministry often tell me I haven't changed. Now, I've grown and matured, but what would I ever change to? Why would I want to be bewitched? Not me! No, I want to grow in the truth that I know and I want to learn new truths every day.

I read the Bible all the time. I get fresh revelation from it and it really blesses me. I thoroughly enjoy walking through the pages of holy writ. I just love it and while I'm walking through it, God is continually teaching me.

I don't know it all, by any means, but I'm ever learning. I believe that if Jesus tarries and I go by the way of the grave, the very day I die I'm going to learn something about Christ. I'm going to learn something about *"...in Him dwelleth all the fullness of the Godhead bodily."*

You see, no one can ever outgrow Christ. The minute I think I have a scripture totally and completely understood, something new comes flying out of God's Spirit into mine and cuts a new facet of understanding onto the jewel of that Word. I want the genetically altered traditions to fall by the wayside so that I can see the real truth and help others know it too.

## Why Write Against Faith?

If you don't think genetically altered Christianity is fighting back, all you have to do is take a drive to the bookstore and see the books written *against* faith. When I first became a Christian, I would have never thought people would spend time writing against something that the Bible expressly says pleases God. It blew my mind when books began declaring *faith* to be some kind of heresy.

How could a Christian be against faith? Isn't that the foundation of everything? Without faith you can't even get saved. You must believe that God exists, that He sent His only begotten Son to die for your sins, that Jesus Christ rose on the third day and now is in Heaven making intercession for you—in other words, He's praying for you!

What do you think Jesus is praying about? I think that He regularly must be praying for us to have *more* faith—because if you go back and read the Gospels, you will see Jesus instructing people to have faith over and over again.

Faith itself was a crucial part of Christ's teachings and He often rebuked people for not having it, and urged them to have more.

So, I don't know how Christians can think they are doing God some kind of favor by writing books and speaking against faith—some call it a great seduction, but if so then who is the seducer? God Himself?! The only thing I can deduce is that they are *not* interested in following Christ and what He taught—they are most interested in maintaining the philosophies and traditions of men.

I don't know why they get so mad at me. I just want to believe what Jesus said and I'm endeavoring to teach the revelations He has given me over the years—and faith is one of them.

Faith has worked for me! I mean, when's the last time you saw me sick as a dog? When's the last time you saw me broke and busted? When's the last time you saw me trying to hurt people? I've been to thousands and thousands of churches and been on television for a long, long time. When's the last time you heard me desperate for money saying, "Won't you help me, won't you help me?! If I don't hear from you today, I'm going off the air!"

---

I'm not bragging on myself! I'm bragging on God—because He sent His Son not only to *die* but also to teach us how to *live*. Faith works! I don't understand preachers who use the pulpit as a weapon. My goal when I preach is to stir people up so that they can live an overcoming life. That's why I don't come with a big stick to beat people. I don't use the Word as a way to abuse them or hurt them. No, I want to bring encouragement!

You will never hear me side with the traditions of men and say something like, "The Lord going to beat you, bust you and stomp you and kick your brains out, but if you endureth to the end, you will be saved!"

That is a genetically altered statement, a twist on the Word of God. No! Christianity is not something I have to *endure*. It's something I get to *enjoy*. I want the world to know that. We don't have to live by the traditions of men.

That doesn't mean the devil doesn't fight me. Of course he fights me! But, what has kept me all these years is this shield of faith. I keep it in front of my face. I'm not like some Christians who are always moving their shield around—bringing it up only when they are under heavy attack and lowering it when things seem OK.

It's as if they are saying "I wonder if the devil is gone? I think I'm gonna look!" Then they poke their head round and *wham!* They get hit with a fiery dart. Your shield of faith ought to be up every day. Leave it up in front of your face.

*"Above all, taking the shield of faith, wherewith ye shall be able to quench all the fiery darts of the wicked"* (Ephesians 6:16). Notice it says "above all." That ought to let you know that faith is important.

# CHAPTER 19

# *Christianity Builds Walls,*
# *Christ Does Not*

One day I was reading the parable of the Prodigal Son and the Lord showed me something. Now, I thought I knew everything there was to know about the story, but as I was sitting there, the Lord spoke to me.

"You are prejudice towards the elder boy," He said, "Your traditions have made you prejudice against him. He was a good *son*. The problem was that he wasn't a good *brother*." That hit me between the eyes. It hit me as revelation. Suddenly, He simply said, "Are you your brother's keeper?"

The first son thought he could live without the father. I'm paraphrasing but he basically said, "Let me run my own way." The second son felt like he was entitled. He was like, "Excuse me? I've served you well, Daddy, and I want you to love me more than you love him."

Notice that the father gave the prodigal son his portion, but he told the elder son, "Everything I've got is here and it's yours. You want me to be a respecter of persons and I cannot be."

You see, the traditions of men tell us that what we do—our works—make us better than other people. No, we are not. "Am I my brother's keeper?" The answer is yes. We are called to be in unity, not division with our brothers and sisters in Christ. So, it's not good to use our works as a way of ranking ourselves and others. It's not our job to judge. That's God's job.

You see, the elder did have a good heart. He did a lot of right things. He was a good son. Yet, we remember him only for being a bad brother. Each of us is a mixed bag and we all have flaws, but God wants us to realize that all our good works mean nothing unless we show love.

## It's Nothing Without Love

God *is* love. He is the foundation of our faith. So, when you show love to others—even those who don't deserve it, *especially* those who don't deserve it like the prodigal son—you are actually showing who God *is* to someone who is as lost as a goose in the fog. Your love literally will pave the way for them to have a greater understanding of God.

If the elder son had shown love, he would have been both a wonderful son and a wonderful brother. But, he got angry, felt more important, and he didn't show any love and that's why we don't ever really remember how good of a son he really was.

Love is the right thing to do. If it feels wrong, it's usually just because our flesh wants to be more important, like the elder son. The flesh is prideful and self-serving. It wants to take instead of give and it wants all the credit all the time. It is greedy and never satisfied. But, when we sow to the spirit and put our faith in God, we don't live according to the flesh.

When we live by the spirit, we understand that God loves us and is going to take care of us regardless of what others around us do. That's when our faith in God calms our flesh to the point that we don't feel the need to cut others down in order to lift ourselves up. That faith in God literally helps us to show love.

You see, it doesn't matter what others get. If you know God loves you, why be jealous? Why be judgmental of someone else's situation? I believe God wants us to be in *cooperation* with one another and not in *competition* with one another. Love causes us to cooperate with our fellow brothers and sisters in God. Fear causes us to compete with one another.

If we do not fight internally for unity, regardless of what others do or believe, our own human nature will cause us to become angry and divisive...and I don't believe God wants His body to be that way.

Unity is a Force

Unity is a spiritual force. Each of us is a link in God's chain. And because of our choice to serve Christ, we always will be linked together. It starts here and never will end because we are going to live together forever in Heaven. So, as they say, a chain is only as strong as the weakest link and whatever we allow to divide us weakens us. Since we're going to live in unity in Heaven in the end, we might as well start doing it right here on earth.

I preach in all types of circles and I'm always being confronted with different points of view that challenge my own. I remember a man once asking me, "What camp are you in?" He wanted to know what category I fell into within the modern, segregated Church.

I told him, "Well, let me just change your question," and added, "There's only *one* camp of God—but there are *many* different colored tents!" He laughed, but he got the point. I don't mind discussing differences but, at the end of the day, the only side we should be taking is God's and He's put us into one "camp"—His own.

You see, we act as if our Father is not the same God, but He *is*. We act as if we aren't going to the same place when we die, but we *will*. God isn't going to segregate Heaven for us. If we can't get along here, then, who knows what happens next? Do we really want to fight each other forever? Do we really want to let our differences divide us?

When you've had real peace, the last thing you want to do is fight over things that don't really matter—instead of looking for ways to disagree, you look for ways to agree, even if it boils down to one thing. You're willing to let that be enough.

I think *Jesus* is enough. If we are believers, it means we believe He is the Son of God, crucified and raised, able to save us and make us one body. Of course, just "not fighting" isn't real peace. You can not fight and still have a whole lot of "fight" left in you.

Peace—the kind I'm talking about—is at the soul level. It's an effect of God that settles down into your soul. With that kind of peace inside, the *gain* of fighting with others in the body of Christ isn't worth the *price* of the fight. Warring with your own people becomes the last thing you want to do.

## I Don't Care About Denominations

I believe that, as a Christian, I ought to be able to preach in any Christian denomination. I mean, if they ask me, then why not do it? What's stopping me? My doctrine? My tradition? Their tradition? I believe that there is always something we can agree upon. I believe I should be able to preach the Word and share my views, as long as it is done in love. If love covers a multitude of sins, surely it should cover a multitude of denominational doctrines.

Look around your town and you'll see how much we've divided our own body. There is little that joins us together at all. We've got Episcopalians, Presbyterians, Catholics, Pentecostals, Baptists and Methodists. We've got people who call themselves by things like Church of God, Church of Christ, Full Gospel, Word of Faith, Assembly of God...we've got so many *names*. I could just keep going and going.

There's a church on just about every corner in some cities and some of them take up whole blocks. But they're not as full as they used to be and some are flat empty. This should not be.

God told me in the earliest years of my ministry that He would open doors for me and He has. I've been asked to preach in wonderful Catholic churches. I've spoken in all sorts of denominations and even outside of Christianity, in Jewish synagogues. I've been blessed to be able to cross many lines. One time, a great black pastor told me, "Jesse, you can get away with saying things in my church that no white man has ever been able to get away with." We talked about it for a little while and then he told me, "It's because they know you love them." That blessed me to my core.

I do love them! Regardless of race, doctrine, or tradition, I love the people. I have to admit that I especially love the black culture. I like that they respond to you and I just enjoy their ways.

You see, it doesn't matter what kind of church I'm in, I want to be an encouragement. I want to speak the truth in love so that the people understand and get that God is on their side—that He wants the best for them. He wants them to come out of bondage and be free, but He wants them to get that way through love and faith instead of a beating from the pulpit!

We don't have to agree on everything to love one another. If we wait to agree, we'll be waiting for eternity. No, God calls us to love now, today, in spite of all our differences.

I often say that God didn't call us to uniformity, but He did call us to unity. So, I don't care if the people I'm preaching to believe a totally genetically altered version of Christianity, I can still preach the truth in love. Even if they don't all accept it, even if we are not in uniformity, the people will still hear me if they know that I love them. We don't have to agree on everything to have unity.

## I'm Not a Methodist, but Jesus Is!

You know, Christianity builds walls, but Christ doesn't. In fact, if you are open, I believe He can use you to show the power of love and unity…even with those that aren't in your "camp" so to speak.

One day I was jogging and I ran by a Methodist Church I'd seen every day for years. As I ran by, I felt the Lord say, "Jesse, go give them a donation."

"Jesus, I'm not a Methodist," I said.

"I am," He said. I almost stopped running right at that second.

I realized something right then and there. Do Methodists love God? Do they believe in Jesus? Yes, they most certainly do.

Well, I finished my jog, came back and took a shower and I told Cathy I wanted to give $5000 to the Methodists. Cathy had her secretary, who is her sister, go over to the church and give the donation.

Now, I want you to see how the traditions of men affect people. Cathy's sister walks into the Methodist church office and says, "Hi, I work for Jesse Duplantis Ministries and Brother Jesse sent me to tell you the Lord spoke to him to give you this money for whatever you need for your church."

The lady looked at her and immediately said the same thing I did, "But he's not Methodist." When Christine told me that, it blew me away—our traditions affect the way we think and they govern what we do, until we allow God to bust us out of what is manmade in the first place. But, we've got to be open to hear Him.

We have built many walls in Christianity. One of those walls was my opinion that I should only support those who think just like I do, but that is wrong. That wall fell over when I was jogging that day.

Now, what I didn't know was that the church was in a building program to add additional structures to the backside of their property. Well, someone told me that the program had stagnated and people weren't giving much to it anymore, yet there was still a need. They told me that the Methodist pastor told the whole congregation the very next Sunday morning and you could see the thought in their mind: *He isn't Methodist.*

Our donation stimulated their joy and it also stimulated the church's building program—because we gave towards it and we weren't even a part of the church, it rekindled a fire in the congregation to get behind the project with more force. They began to give again and built their building.

Now, what was stopping their building project? I believe it was the traditions of men—it was what got thrown aside the day I jogged by and decided to be my brother's keeper. That day I became a good brother and a good son. That day, I made my Father proud.

# CHAPTER 20

# The "Rudiments" of the World

*Beware lest any man spoil you through philosophy and vain deceit, after the tradition of men, after the rudiments of the world, and not after Christ.*

Colossians 2:8

So, what does the word *rudiment* mean? The dictionary defines a rudiment as a basic principle or element, or a fundamental skill. It is something unformed and undeveloped. When the Word says to beware that you are not "spoiled" by the "rudiments of the world" it is warning you not to fall into the trap of thinking and acting according to the basic principles of this world—to instead live Christ's way. In other words, we may be *in* this world, but as believers we are not *of* this world.

There is a fundamental difference between a believer and an unbeliever and it is the light of God that opens our eyes to the truth. But what happens when believers themselves let go and stop letting that light of God illuminate their lives? What happens when they lose sight of the truth and just start going through the motions?

I'll tell you what happens…the "rudiments of the world" is what happens! Suddenly, relationship with Christ takes a back seat and distortion starts rolling in full force. Christ stops being the issue. Everything becomes a "concept" to explore, instead of a life to be lived.

### Rudiments and Religion, Wilderness and Weeds

It doesn't matter if something has been taught for hundreds or even thousands of years, if it is not God's way, it's not the right way. If it smacks up against Christ's way—the only *true* way—then we must recognize it for what it is, *"…philosophy vain deceit after the tradition of men, after the rudiments of the world, and not after Christ"* (Colossians 2:8).

When people tell me, "you never know what God is going to do." I can't help myself from saying, "What does the Word say about it?" Oh, they get mad! You see, to them, it really doesn't make a difference what the Word actually says. What matters is their opinion about what they've read, which is usually convoluted by the rudiments of the world. But, my life isn't based on opinions of men; it's based upon the Word of the living God.

I look at them like, "Do you want me to accept the rudiments of the world over the Word of the Living God? Really? I don't care if everyone's done it for two thousand years; I'm not going to do that!" Why? Because it's just a distorted religious concept. It's an altered biblical doctrine and if I live by that junk, I'm not going to excel in any way—I'm going to live and die sick, broke, and sad and I don't want to do that!

**The "rudiments of the world" are at the heart of man's genetically altered biblical doctrines and distorted religious concepts.**

Religion is a theological wilderness. It's a garden of weeds. It never produces anything other than pure works, which are good but God meant them to be mixed with faith. Without that heart element, it will always be lacking.

Religion is like going to a restaurant and ordering wonderful food. But, you never get the food...you only get the bill. That's religion! You order healing and you hear, "Sorry, we're out of that." You order salvation for your family and hear, "Oh, I'm sorry, we're out of that too."

Religion is just a list of dos and don'ts without any power whatsoever. Oh, you're told to order, but you're also told not to *expect* anything in return. So, you end up with nothing. That is not the way of Christ. That is not how He lived His life or how He taught us to live ours. It's the "rudiments of the world" way.

## Dedicating My Baby

Even as a sinner, I had respect for God in my own way. Although I didn't want to personally serve God, when my baby was born, I found myself wanting to have somebody pray over her as an infant—I wanted my baby to have that formal ceremony of being dedicated to God. Something about her innocence wanted me to keep her innocent, and the only way I knew how to give her that start was to ask God for His blessing on my child.

Now, I was a heathen from hell! But, you see, something inside of me even back then knew that n all my intellectual activity, my range and research and my induction and reasoning were flawed—God was bigger than my opinions about Him.

When Cathy asked me, "Really, you want to dedicate the baby?"

I said, "Yeah, we've GOT to do that."

She looked at me and couldn't believe I wanted to do it. I was a rock musician, drinking heavily and on drugs. She looked at me like, *But Jesse, you don't even care about God, you're a heathen from hell!*

I later realized that I thought alot like Michael Corleone from The Godfather movie when he got his baby christened. I can see the scene from the movie in my head. The baby being christened and the words, "Michael, do you denounce Satan?" *Boom, boom, boom* of the gun. His response, "Yes."

Well, I wasn't Michael Corleone, but I'm just saying that's a good picture of how I believed back then—you live one way and you tell your kids to live another because you know your way isn't good. Religion just doesn't change people.

## *Lying and Drunk…In Church*

I mean the way I saw it, you went to church and if you had to go to the confessional…well, you lied. When I say this sometimes in a sermon, you can see the Catholics in the room just about pass out from shock. I tell them, "Don't look at me like you're innocent. You know you went to confession and you lied too!"

If I ask people, "How many of y'all lied? Hold your hand up! Come on, admit it!" Catholics all over the building will smile a little and throw up their hand for a split-second, like they're afraid a lightening bolt is going to come through the roof and hit them on the forehead.

Why did we all lie, mostly lies of omission? Because we wanted to get out with just three "Hail Marys" and three "Our Father" prayers! So, we'd say, "Bless me father for I have sinned it's been 'X' days since my last confession." That was the first lie because we didn't confess on regular basis and we didn't want to admit it—a typical "3 weeks" in the X-slot sounded better than "over a year."

One time, I'll never forget I decided to tell the truth. I started talking and I just kept going. I unloaded so much sin that the priest thought I was pulling his leg and literally said, "Awww, come on!" He couldn't believe it. The priest actually went against the rules and got out of his side of the confessional, and opened the door to my side of the box to get a good look at me. I bet he hadn't heard a true confession in years.

Now, if you were Baptist, things were totally different. There wasn't a priest to confess to at the Baptist church, so you just lied at the altar. You'd go up and say, "Oh God, forgive me!" Then, five minutes later, you went back to doing the same thing. You maybe didn't even figure it mattered, because in your mind, once you were saved you were always saved, and so sin stopped mattering as much. In other words, religion itself didn't have the power to change you.

If you were Pentecostal, things were even more different. I can't tell you how many people I've seen leave a power-packed service where they spoke in tongues and rolled around on the floor and just looked like they were walking the halls of glory...and then, get so angry that they cuss in the parking lot because somebody cut them off as they were trying to leave the church.

Sometimes in my meetings in Louisiana, where the majority religion is Catholic, I ask, "How many of y'all went to midnight mass drunk?" You should see the people! They laugh and snicker and some even have the guts to raise their hands.

If I ask them to stand up if they ever did it, you'd be shocked at how many people are coming up from those pews. Why? Because we partied on Christmas eve, but as Catholics we still made sure we showed up for midnight mass. What was happening there? I'll tell you! It was genetically altered Christianity. That's not a shot against the Catholics because that same thing was happening across the board throughout the varied denominations of Christianity.

It's called the rudiments of the world! It's the basic principles of the world infiltrating our lives to such a degree that even God's Word and His ways fall by the wayside when push comes to shove.

If you think you're the only one who has lived this way, you're not—it's been going on for over two thousand years since the beginning of Christianity. That's because religion in and of itself doesn't bring you any closer to God. How many times have you gone to church feeling good and left feeling bad? It's epidemic.

## It's Not Just a Book, It's Something Living

Before I became a Christian, I didn't really think that much about God. I wouldn't say I was an atheist, but I was growing agnostic. I figured God might be out there but I didn't think He was directly involved in people's lives and so, I thought it was pointless to talk about Him.

Besides that, I had grown up in all sorts of churches and come to the opinion that it didn't work anyway. As a kid, it seemed like everybody who believed in healing was sick. Everybody who talked about being blessed was broke. And the same people who talked about the love of God still hated other people in the church.

On one hand, they would say that Jesus was the Lord of their life and on the other hand, they were prejudice against people whose skin was a different color than their own. I didn't understand it as a kid. It didn't make any sense. I asked myself why I should adhere to some religion that didn't work. So, I didn't. After all, I figured that if it didn't work for them, it sure wouldn't work for me.

I came to view the Bible as a historical document filled with great moral stories—something that was supposed to breed good character and integrity. They called it "The Good Book" and I agreed that it had great moral concepts, but I just wasn't interested in them. Then, of course, I met the true Author…the one that inspired the Word. And when I met Jesus, the Person, and accepted His love and sacrifice, all that religion I grew up on came under question.

I wanted truth but even after I became a Christian, I found myself naturally falling into my old ideas about the Bible and God. You see, I tried range and research. I tried induction and reasoning. I remembered ideas from my childhood and those old ideas wrapped themselves around whatever I heard preached—they influenced how I "heard" the Word.

So, then, I did something different. I began to read the Bible for *myself.* I opened not only my mind to what it actually said, but I allowed the Holy Spirit living inside of me to guide me. John 16:13 became real to me, *"Howbeit when He, the Spirit of truth, is come, He will guide you into all truth…"*

As I read the Bible with this new openness, I found out that it was not a book—it was something *living.* Jesus became not only the author of my newfound faith, but the finisher. I knew He was working on me, not only on my heart but my head, and I began to view things in a different light.

So, all my old induction, reasoning, range, and research begin to fail me because I couldn't get them to come together. They were just opinions and not John 16:13 Spirit-led truth. I believe that if the Bible had been any other book, it wouldn't have changed me.

## The Galatians Had A Problem With It Too

Your highest development is being "in Christ"—because the best you are ever going to be is when you are allowing Him to live through you, instead of living according to your own ways. If you struggle, you have something in common with the church at Galatians.

*"Even so we, when we were children, were in bondage under the elements of the world"* (Galatians 4:3). In other words, the Galatians felt like there was a time when they too were living under the elements, or rudiments, of the world.

**The philosophic mind never reaches it's highest development until it is "Christ-ianized."**

We don't serve Chris. We serve Christ. You must become "Christ-ianized" to the point that you are no longer subservient to a set of religious rules, but you are serving Jesus—the anointed one—Christ. It is a heart principle that sets you apart from others who are simply going through the motions.

My birth name is Jesse Duplantis, but now that I serve Christ, I have been adopted into God's family and my name has an added word, "Christian!" I like to say I'm a *Christ*-ian; not a *Chris*-tian. I'm in the family of Christ, not Chris. That's why Satan hates me. It'll be the same reason he hates you.

Still, it's worth all his scorn because there is no higher way to live than to serve Jesus—the One who loved you enough to die for you. I can't share this point enough. Your mind *has* to become Christianized in order for you to reach your highest developmental potential as a person. No other code of living compares!

## The Total Source

You can't live Christ's way without His Spirit living through you. Think about it. Have you ever read the scripture about the fruit of the Spirit? Did you notice how impossible it seems to have all these attributes...on your own? That's why they are called "fruit" of the "Spirit"—you've got to have the Spirit moving through you in order to produce any of them. You must be close to the "fruit tree."

*"But the fruit of the Spirit is love, joy, peace, longsuffering, gentleness, goodness, faith, meekness, temperance: against such there is no law. And they that are Christ's have crucified the flesh with the affections and lusts. If we live in the Spirit, let us also walk in the Spirit"*

Galatians 5:22-25

Notice, it takes living in the Spirit to walk in the Spirit. It's not a Sunday thing. If it's just that religious obligation, there is no way you will ever be able to produce these kinds of fruit.

I've had really famous preachers ask me why I am consistently producing joy. One of them, who you'd know if I mentioned his name, said, "I just don't understand why you are so happy. I guess I didn't get saved like you."

I couldn't help myself. I said, "Well, maybe you're not."

Oh, he got as hot as a pistol. He was mad! Why? Because his total source of supply is not God. Its people—the love of the people, the attention of the people, and continual support of the people. But, at the end of the day, I don't care how great of a preacher or a person you are, if your total source of supply isn't God, you will not be joyful—because that is a fruit of His Spirit and you only get it by doing it His way, living in Christ.

God sent His Son for a reason beyond salvation. He also sent Him to help you enjoy and produce love, joy, peace, longsuffering, gentleness, goodness, faith, meekness, and temperance. There isn't a law on this earth that forbids them because everyone notices them as good.

# CHAPTER 21

# I'm Not For Sale

Some preachers are wonderful speakers and they can move people emotionally, but if they do it and rely on people, they do not have God as their total source of supply. So, no matter what, the money and the prestige will run out as quickly as the peace and the joy. That's a fact!

Why? Because emotionalism can't take the place of the anointing. It's a cheap substitute. It's "the elements of the world." It's "the rudiments of the world." It's a way other than God's way, and its religious bondage.

When I see preachers do this, it irritates me. I'm not against raising money, but the church and its leaders shouldn't be just raising money…we ought to be *giving* money too. Sowing and reaping is not something that only the *people* should just do. Giving should be across the board because sowing and reaping is a message for *all*.

As long as the earth remains, sowing and reaping will be part of God's system. It's just as sure as the rest of the things He placed in effect. Genesis 8:22, *"While the earth remains, seedtime and harvest, cold and heat, winter and summer, and day and night shall not cease."*

## What Is Church Even For?!

Do you ever wonder why you go to church? I don't think of the local church as some religious self-help gathering. I think of it as part and parcel of Christ—a place where His "body" comes together for a purpose.

Some Christians treat church like a rock concert. If there is a guest speaker, they will come see the "star" do his or her thing, but you can barely get them to go on a regular basis because the pastor just isn't exciting enough for them. That bothers me because it shows that a lot of people have the wrong idea about it.

Church is more than spiritual entertainment—it's a place to get spiritually nourished and also to give what you've got to those around you. Hebrews 10:24-25 puts it this way, *"And let us consider one another to provoke unto love and to good works: Not forsaking the assembling of ourselves together, as the manner of some is; but exhorting one another: and so much the more, as ye see the day approaching."*

In other words, when we come together at church, we should come with a mindset to "provoke" each other to love and do good things. That means we can stimulate one another to do right before we ever hear a word from the pulpit. It means church is collaborative.

So, it isn't just a place to get something, it's a place to *give* something to others. I'm not just talking about the offering time. I'm talking about the moment you walk through the doors. That moment, even before, you should be giving and receiving. You see, your face matters. Your smile matters. Your words matter. Who do they matter to? To God and to the other people who are there. *You* matter.

Again, church is collaborative. We are a body, fitted together for the purpose of gathering people to Christ through love and good works, and provoking one another through the same two things.

When people come into a church that way, it is easy for God to move. When Christ, the King of Kings, is at every service, man, the anointing just flows! And in His presence there is direction for our lives and a fullness of joy that is hard to explain—it makes church more of a pleasure and less of a lesson in endurance. Psalms 16:11, *"Thou wilt shew me the path of life: in Thy presence is fullness of joy; at thy right hand there are pleasures for evermore."*

Now, don't get me wrong. I love guest speakers. I love excitement. I love great preaching. But, my point is this. I go to church simply because I'm hungry for what God has, no matter who He uses to get the message across, and I just plain want to be in the house of God with other believers. I need people the same way people need me. It's how God made humanity.

Isolation breeds all sorts of trouble. We are created to be a part of one another's lives. Church is a great place to gather together. It's a heart issue and when the heart is right, God will always give you something and always use you to give something to someone else.

Look, when I first got saved I knew that I was in a battle! Life had done a number on me—anger, drugs, alcoholism, you name it. Oh, I had been financially successful, but I was flat broke on the inside. I was spiritually destitute and impoverished. So, I knew that after I received Christ, I needed to learn some things! I needed some tools on how to live this life. I knew I needed some weaponry to fight the battles that were at my door. And I knew that the only place

I could get those kinds of spiritual principles was at God's house... until they genetically altered it on me!

A genetically altered Christianity robs people from the spiritual weapons and the spiritual blessings they need in order to succeed God's way in life—which is why a philosophical mind can never reach its highest development until it is Christianized. We need *Christ* to succeed.

## Searching for a Feeling

Another genetically altered thing I hear in a lot of church circles is the need to get "fresh oil"...as if the Holy Spirit Himself gets stale now and then. It's a concept that comes from a genetically altered Bible! When I hear people say this, what I think they are really saying is, "I've got to feel something again." Man, even the *devil* can make you feel something! So feelings can't be your guide as to whether the Holy Spirit is moving or not.

Even a demon can give you a "word" and try to make you think you are hearing the voice of God—they sometimes masquerade as an angel of light. There are many familiar spirits that know human nature. They also have the ability to know a lot about you if they decide to study you and some will do just that. Their goal is to mess with you and draw you away from God. It's really not about *you*. They just want to hurt God. Since you mean something to God, that makes you worth attacking.

So you must renew your mind to the scripture so you know the Word—this is what you fight Satan with. The Word is your spiritual weapon. You must also know the voice of the Lord so you don't go off track by following something else.

Jesus said, *"My sheep hear My voice, and I know them, and they follow Me."* (John 10:27). Notice Jesus didn't say you are to follow your feelings. No, He said *"...I know them, and they follow Me."* Christianity is not about following a religious set of rules just as much as it is not about following "feelings" of God and goosebumps—it's about following JESUS.

You may need to draw closer to Jesus. You may need to get rid of sin by repenting and asking His forgiveness so that your prayers aren't hindered. But you don't need "fresh oil." The Christ you serve is fresh all the time—He is enough and He will always stay the same. *"Jesus Christ the same yesterday, and today, and forever"* (Hebrews 13:8).

## I'm Not For Sale

Now, I love excitement at church. It's fun! But, you've got to understand the difference between entertainment and the anointing. There's nothing wrong with being entertained. Its fun and inspiring maybe, but it can't change your spiritual walk. So, if you don't recognize the difference, you can be led by emotion and somebody can take advantage of you. Don't let anybody snow you!

I'll never forget when I really learned this lesson. I was a very young preacher in the 1970s and a pastor had booked me in a series of meetings they were holding. I believe it was a Sunday through Friday campmeeting. Well, I was scheduled for Thursday and when I got there, the pastor told me that the offerings hadn't been very good. Then, he made sure to tell me that he wanted me to play the piano—a lot. Back then, I played piano just as much as I preached so it wasn't unusual to have a request, but what he said to me just about blew me away.

"Jesse, we want you to play some of that Jerry Lee and Mickey Gilley stuff. We want you to kick that piano, kick that piano stool out! Man, we'll throw a cup of gasoline on you to start a fire if we have to, just kick it out! And then, we're going to hit them up for an offering!" Those were his exact words. My mouth fell open but instead of protesting, I got an idea.

"Can I receive the offering tonight?" I asked.

He was thrilled and said, "Oh, would you do it for us?"

"I would love to," I said.

Well, I got out there and buddy, I prayed before I even touched the piano keys, "Lord, heal my fingers. I'm gonna bust these fingers up in a few minutes and blood is going to be flying but I'm gonna tear this piano up."

I sat down and I went to kicking it out! I played hard and fast. I gave it every ounce of energy and sweat I had. I did exactly what the man asked of me. I gave him my best Jerry Lee Lewis piano playing. Sweat was running down my legs and I sang strong and loud, did entertaining as if I still did it for a living. Even the piano started going out, I was busting the strings and I saw a few fly out.

Man, I jumped on top of it and hit the keys with my shoe like that old piano man, Jerry Lee Lewis! I kicked that piano stool out, just like he asked me to do. The people were going crazy. I mean had them on their feet screaming and that's when I did it.

"You know," I told the frenzied crowd, "We *were* going to receive an offering tonight! But, we don't need any money! So, we aren't receiving anything tonight! We've got enough! Sit down, let's just have some fun!" The pastor almost passed out cold. I finished playing. I walked off that stage and as I did, I looked that pastor straight in the eye and said, "I'm not for sale. And don't you ever make me a part of trying to hype somebody up so you can get their money."

I was disgusted by the whole thing. You see, that's genetically altered religion at work.

I also told him, "I am not paying for your piano either!" Oh, I tore up it up, but I didn't care. Well, one thing is for certain. After that night, the pastor never asked me to come back to his church!

## I Love Being Free

I enjoy being free. John 8:36 says, *"If the Son therefore shall make you free, ye shall be free indeed."* Being free isn't just about Jesus taking away your sins. It's about trusting in Him enough to do what you must do in any given situation.

When you understand your freedom, you can literally be around sinners who are really bad and not fall into acting like them. Why? Because you understand 1 John 4:4, *"Ye are of God, little children, and have overcome them: because greater is He that is in you, than he that is in the world."*

You know that Who is on the inside of you is greater than the one inside of them. Jesus is ENOUGH. He is the One who freed you. He is the One who will keep you and cause you to be able overcome anything. Again, it's about following the Person and not the religion.

## Even a Sinner Can Whip the Devil

Even a baby Christian can whip the devil. In fact, do you know that, even as a sinner, you probably whipped the devil a few times? Remember, his goal is never just to irritate you…his goal is to do three things: kill, steal, and destroy, and not necessarily in that order.

*"The thief cometh not, but for to steal, and to kill, and to destroy: I am come that they might have life, and that they might have it more abundantly"* (John 10:10).

How many times, before you were saved, were you drinking, smoking dope, going crazy and you hear a voice inside say, "Let's go out and get even drunker, let's go do more drugs, mess around some more, and do a few lines more..."? And how many times, instead of agreeing, did you say, "Nah, I ain't doing that, I'm tired, I'm going home. I'm going to bed, I'm just tired"?

Do you realize that every single time you backed off from going further into sin, you beat the devil? Every time you chose to take it down a notch, you beat the devil. Because his goal was never just to make sure you had a good time. That was his bait.

His ultimate goal was always to kill, steal, and destroy your life. He always wanted to push you one step closer to one of those three things, and maybe all, because that is his goal. So, even as a sinner, you shut him down every time you didn't take your sin to the end of the wire.

Well, if you can shut him down as a sinner, don't you think you can shut him down as a Christian? Let the elevator go to the top!

## You Don't Have to Sin Every Day That's Genetically Altered!

When I was growing up, I often heard people say, "Well, you know, you have to ask for forgiveness every day because you are going to sin every day. We're all just sinners saved by grace." As I grew in the Lord as an adult, I came to realize that this was a totally genetically altered statement...and tons of people believed it as holy truth!

Do you have to sin every day? NO! Yes, Romans 3:23 is point blank blunt and true: *"For all have sinned, and come short of the glory of God."* Have is past tense. In other words, we've all done it… but we don't have to keep doing it forever!

There are many passages that talk about how we've sinned but the Bible doesn't say we are all "sinners" forever either. I don't sin every day and I don't believe you have to either. You see, we *were* sinners before we knew God. But, our status changes the moment we accept Christ—that's when we are saved by grace and are no longer "sinners" but are "the righteous." The blood of Jesus did that for us and nothing else.

One of my favorite passages is what Paul said about Himself in Galatians 2:20-21, *"I am crucified with Christ: nevertheless I live; yet not I, but Christ liveth in me: and the life which I now live in the flesh I live by the faith of the Son of God, who loved me, and gave Himself for me. I do not frustrate the grace of God: for if righteousness come by the law, then Christ is dead in vain."*

In other words, after we accept Jesus, it's up to us what we will do every day. If we see ourselves (our flesh) as "crucified with Christ" and we are letting Christ live *in* us and *through* us each day, then we won't get into a state of constantly sinning. Consequently, we won't *"frustrate the grace of God"* as Paul puts it.

What do you think frustrates God's grace? Continuing to live in a perpetual state of sin. It's when you don't care that the tools you need to live right are at your disposal, and you continue on giving in to the flesh. That is frustrating to God.

So, no, you don't have to sin every day. That's a genetically altered viewpoint! Yes, you may sin and, yes, you may fall—and God's grace and mercy is always there for you when you choose to ask forgiveness and repent—but *you* are the righteousness of Christ

Jesus now and *you* have the ability to live much of your life *not* sinning.

## Going A Long Time Without Sinning

You know, I go long extended periods of time without sinning. In fact, there are times when I almost have to *make* myself sin because it's become so uncommon in my life. The only time I do it is when I'm in the flesh, but I've found that if I crucify my flesh daily, instead of Sunday—if I stay *Christ*ianized instead of religiously *Christ*ianized—I won't fulfill the lusts of the flesh. You see, I can't combat the flesh with religion; only through my relationship with Christ can I truly conquer my own flesh nature.

My wife Cathy is good at stopping me from sinning. I think my greatest weakness is my temper. I'm hot-blooded and can be impatient. When I get mad, I want to knock the fire out of something. Since my wife knows me so well, she can see when I start to get hot under the collar and trys to calm me down before I let the flesh take me where I don't really want to go.

It's good to have people in your life that can help you...even if you don't always listen to them! At least, they are on God's side saying, "C'mon! Don't frustrate His grace today!"

# CHAPTER 22

# Beware of Lofty Intellectualism

A lot of people who have been believers for a while get tired of the simple truths of Christianity and that often leads to genetically altered truths. Beware of lofty intellectualism when it comes to the Word of God. It can darken your true understanding. If you exchange faith in God's power for intellectualism, it can pollute your conscience and worst of all, weaken your will.

Your will is the most powerful *natural* thing you've got. Your mind, will, and emotions can spiral down quickly. So, it's important not to let anything come in and weaken your will in life.

Childlike faith is fearless faith. A person with child-like faith doesn't split hairs about God. He recognizes the grandness of God and simply believes. He knows that God can do anything and His Word is good. Like Abraham, a person with child-like faith is fully persuaded that whatever God has promised, He is also able to perform (Romans 4:21).

## Albert Einstein and God

A lot of people don't think of lofty intellectualism as something that infects believers. They think it only relates to highly educated theorists and philosophers, but that's not true. The mindset of throwing aside the simple truth about God in favor of a convoluted mix of uncertainties has threaded its fingers throughout society.

I find it amazing that one of the most admired intellectuals, Albert Einstein, did not throw aside faith in God even though, in his circles, believing in God was looked down upon. Now, he didn't believe many things the Church believed at the time, but he talked about God often and had to defend the fact that he was not an atheist his whole life through.

I love some of his quotes about God like: "Before God we are all equally wise and equally foolish," and "Science without religion is lame, religion without science is blind." "My religion consists of humble admiration of the illimitable superior Spirit who reveals Himself in the slight details we are able to perceive with our frail and feeble mind." But, again, my all-time favorite Einstein quote is the simple, "God does not play dice."

In other words, while he had a scientific mind, he also had enough humility not to just assume God didn't exist because He hadn't yet been proven to exist by the scientific community. I love that his opinion about God was not based on what he could scientifically define.

You know, you don't have to understand *everything* to believe in *something*. Some things are beyond the scope of what we can see. Einstein saw an intelligent design to the universe and often used the word "order" to reiterate his point, as in the universe is in perfect order. It seems that he believed God put it into that perfect order.

———————

Now, his peers got mad that he didn't give up his belief in God. And even though his was a lofty intellectualism, by saying something like "God does not play dice" he was giving credit to the Creator—and dismissing that everything was about chance. He didn't believe creation was a gamble. They would get so mad at him for talking that way, but since he was the most brilliant one of them all, they couldn't say anything really.

The theory he came up with E=mc2 caused everyone to look at physics in a totally different way, totally different than Newton and all the other great theorists before him…yet he understood "order" and, in fact, was simply trying to catch God at His work. It is a wonderful thing when a brilliant person tries to understand His creator. It becomes something both simple and complex, and ultimately profound. Albert Einstein had enough sense not to let his brilliance make him a fool.

But most people don't do that. Most people aren't that smart. Many who dabble in lofty intellectualism follow the path that chooses to leave God behind—which is why we should beware lofty intellectualism…the kind that exchanges the truth of God for something else.

## Don't Let It Darken Your Understanding, Or Pollute Your Emotions

Lofty intellectualism can darken your true understanding. You can convince yourself of something to such a degree that, even when you see the truth, you refuse to see it and call it a lie. It can pollute your conscience to the point that it is seared and that inner knowing of true right and wrong gets mixed up. Soon right and wrong is conditional upon the situation, but God is not that way. He has clear rights and wrongs and makes them plain.

It can also pollute your emotion. When you spiral away from the simple truth about God—His goodness manifested in Christ and His love and concern for you and your life—when you get away from that and dive into various theories that pull you away from His simple truth, it will drag you off course from the only true source of peace really available to you.

Today, there is this opinion that you can find peace in yourself. That sounds great and you may be able to change your own mind about things but, God, your Creator, can give you something higher than your own conjured up fragmented version of peace.

In Philippians 4:6-7, God gives us a recipe for how to get a better form of peace when it says, *"Be anxious for nothing, but in everything by prayer and supplication, with thanksgiving, let your requests be made known to God; and the peace of God, which surpasses all understanding, will guard your hearts and minds through Christ Jesus."*

Notice, the peace of God is something different than the peace of self. The peace of God comes through humility, bringing your cares to God, making your requests known, and allowing that trust in Him to carve a new way of being in your life. Notice that the peace of God doesn't just bring you calming. It guards your heart and mind. In other words, His peace is protection, not just a divine form of an anti-anxiety pill. And, notice too that the protective peace is *"of God"* but it comes *"through Christ Jesus."*

So, the point is, don't let lofty intellectualism pull you from the One who not only can calm your soul, but has the power to protect it. Don't give the vain philosophies of men the power to steal your peace.

## *Refuse to Allow Anything To Weaken Your Will*

The worst thing of all about lofty intellectualism in my opinion is that it has the potential of weakening your will. I think that's usually the last stage, but, buddy, when your will is weakened, you've got trouble on your hands.

That's how you fall into sin. That's how you mess up and go off course. I can't tell you how many people who once truly loved God went to a phenomenal college and became agnostic! I'm telling you the truth. They couldn't handle the philosophies they heard— they left their faith by the wayside in favor of lofty intellectualism. Look, education and faith are not mutually exclusive! You can have and do both if you want. You don't have to pick! But, it starts with alterations so small you don't even recognize them as harmful... and yet, for many people, it pollutes their faith and distorts their understanding.

Remember, Jesus had all sorts of guys as his disciples. Highly educated and blue collar. Faith doesn't have to be for only a certain group. Romans 12:3 says that God gave all of us a measure of faith. He wants you to use it because He knows that without him, the devil can kick your rear and ruin your destiny.

That's what you call letting the rudiments of the world take the place of the truth of God in your life—and its designed so that Satan can move you whenever he sees fit to do it. You see, lofty intellectualism usually dismisses Satan a lot. Yet, the whole Bible shows us the play between darkness and light.

CHAPTER 23

# Satan Tried Lofty Intellectualism On Jesus

Satan is real and so are the angels who fell along with him. I love 1 Corinthians 14:33 which says, *"For God is not the author of confusion, but of peace, as in all churches of the saints."* In other words, the opposite of peace is confusion, and it doesn't come from God.

So, if God is not the author of confusion, who do you think is? The devil, right? He would like to darken your understanding to such a degree that you turn from your true path. He does it through lofty intellectualism a lot. He tried it on Eve and it worked. He tried it on Jesus…and it didn't.

Read Matthew 4:1-11 to see how the devil talked in tempting Jesus and you'll be able to detect the lofty intellectualism.

*"Then was Jesus led up of the Spirit into the wilderness to be tempted of the devil.*

*"And when He had fasted forty days and forty nights, He was afterward an hungered.*

*"And when the tempter came to Him, he said, If thou be the Son of God, command that these stones be made bread.*

*"But He answered and said, It is written, Man shall not live by bread alone, but by every word that proceedeth out of the mouth of God.*

*"Then the devil taketh Him up into the holy city, and setteth Him on a pinnacle of the temple,*

*"And saith unto Him, If thou be the Son of God, cast thyself down: for it is written, He shall give His angels charge concerning thee: and in their hands they shall bear Thee up, lest at any time Thou dash Thy foot against a stone.*

*"Jesus said unto him, It is written again, Thou shalt not tempt the Lord thy God.*

*"Again, the devil taketh Him up into an exceeding high mountain, and sheweth Him all the kingdoms of the world, and the glory of them;*

*"And saith unto Him, All these things will I give Thee, if Thou wilt fall down and worship me.*

*"Then saith Jesus unto him, Get thee hence, Satan: for it is written, Thou shalt worship the Lord thy God, and him only shalt thou serve.*

*"Then the devil leaveth Him, and, behold, angels came and ministered unto Him.*

Matthew 4:1-11

Notice that, first, he appeals to His pride and His abilities saying something akin to "I thought You were God! You're hungry? Turn the stones to bread! You can create the universe? Show me how You make bread!"

Now, Jesus could have turned that stone into a loaf of bread. He could have made a mountain of bread with a log of butter running down the valley, with pancakes and syrup hanging off the cliffs! He could have done anything He wanted to do. But, Jesus only said, *"Man shall not live by bread alone, but by every Word that proceeds out of the mouth of God."* In other words, "Food is not what fulfills me, God's Word does. I will not perform a godly act in a prideful spirit. NO."

Next, he tried to get Jesus to harm Himself to test God's protection—he was trying to work on Jesus' knowledge of God's love. He basically told Him to throw Himself off a cliff and see if God will save you. Go ahead; give the angels something to do. See if God loves You enough to perform His Word. Jesus dismissed that by speaking scripture, *"Jesus said unto him, It is written again, Thou shalt not tempt the Lord thy God."*

## A Kingdom...Altered

The way Jesus handled the first two temptations blew Satan away and since neither worked, he changed strategies and went right for the thing he thought would pull at Jesus' heart the most. I believe the devil thought, *Wait a minute, let's deal with Jesus' vision. He wants to touch the world. He wants a kingdom. I'm gonna show Him a kingdom! But I'm gonna alter it and it's gonna have money and power!*

So, he takes him up high and, as they look down, the devil basically says, "You want a kingdom? I've got a kingdom! Look, here it is man! Run it like You want. You be the boss, I don't care. All You gotta do (here comes the alteration)…all you have to do is worship me right here. Worship me, nobody even has to know, and You get all this you see and you can run it like you want."

Now, remember, the devil first tried to tempt Jesus with what He really needed, sustenance to survive—*Go ahead, use Your power to provide Yourself some food.* Next, he tried to hurt Him emotionally—*Do you really think God cares about You enough to intervene if You hurt Yourself?* Now, he breaks out the big dog—*If You want what God promised, You can have it, and You can have it ahead of time. Would You take an altered version of Your vision, if it gave You a similar end result? Compromise! C'mon!*

So, everything Satan said meant to bring Jesus down a different track than God's Word or His will—but everything Jesus said was Word-orientated and not genetically altered.

> *"Then saith Jesus unto him, Get thee hence, Satan: for it is written, Thou shalt worship the Lord thy God, and Him only shalt thou serve. Then the devil leaveth Him, and, behold, angels came and ministered unto Him"*

> Matthew 4:10-11

Jesus had enough—*Get out of here, Satan! I'm only worshipping and serving God.* Notice that Jesus refused to enter into a conversation with the devil about His vision. He refused to entertain the notion. Instead, He went right to the heart of the matter. *I'm not serving you, get out!* And the devil, beaten, left and angels came to help and minister to Jesus, Who had just gone through a hard temptation.

You see, it wouldn't be called temptation if it wasn't something that pulled on Christ—and I believe it pulled on Jesus at every level, physically, emotionally, in relation to His bond with the Father, spiritually, and in every way. He wouldn't have needed angels to come and help minister to Him if it wasn't a battle.

Yet, Jesus did what few of us in the same position would do—He refused to accept genetically altered versions of the Word of God, even if it met His immediate needs and dreams for the future. I love that! I hope you do too! I hope you see that in Christ, we have purity of Word and purity of motivation…and in any other path, we have a genetically altered viewpoint that drags us away from core truth and towards all the trappings of Satan.

## If You Beat Him, He'll Leave You For a Season

Sometimes, I see things in the ministry that really bother me. Like these preachers who build churches and get in such financial trouble because they never use good business sense. Then, they fall on their faces and ask God to bail them out. Yes, God is the Author and Finisher of our faith, but He is under no responsibility to finish something He didn't ask you to do and has not authored.

If He chooses to bail you out of a mistake, it's a sovereign act on His part and you better hit your knees in gratitude! But, if He doesn't choose to bail you out, you can't blame Him. You will have to pay for your own mistake—because your choice is a by-product of your own genetically altered Christianity.

Jesus beat the devil at his own game of genetically altered Christianity. And the Bible says the devil left Jesus for a season. He beat him so bad, the devil just left! You see, the uncompromised Word shuts the devil down. He can't argue with truth. He can only manipulate it and attack it. When he knows he's lost, he doesn't hang around to hear more. He's a punk. He's interested in flesh-thinking. So, he'll leave to bother someone else he thinks will twist his way.

Not too long ago, I gave an altar call and about six hundred people came forward to accept Jesus—I beat the devil up so bad that night, he stayed home the whole next day. It was as if he said, "Jesse just beat my brains out. I'm gonna leave him alone in case he tries to beat me more."

You see, he does get tired. He's a flesh devil, fleshly in his way of thinking, but he always comes back. He has to go and rest himself. Again, 1 John 4:4 says it best, *"Ye are of God, little children, and have overcome them: because greater is He that is in you, than he that is in the world."*

Notice how God references us as "little children." We can't beat him in the flesh, but we can beat him with child-like faith in God— we beat him when we know that the Greater One lives in *us*. God in us, working through us, and with His Words coming out of our mouth, is what it takes to beat the devil and his most genetically altered viewpoints of Christianity.

Always remember...he doesn't have a fourth temptation. He is limited. No matter how much he comes at you with lofty intellectualism about God and the Word, if you stick with the pure, un-genetically altered Word of God, he *will* leave you for a season. He can't win when you speak God's truth. Period.

### Nothing Wrong with Philosophy That Comes From Above

There's nothing wrong with philosophy, as long as it comes from wisdom that is from above—and not the fallacy of a genetically altered Bible. The whole reason for this book is because you are going to combat genetically altered "wisdom" all your life, and yet the key to succeeding God's way is having simple, child-like faith in His Word. It's that purity of faith that works best.

I always say, if you want a safety net, look at the Word and ask yourself, "What does the Word say about this situation?" Then, pray it out! Study it! Let the Holy Spirit implant God's truth into your heart. Let it be the simple truth and not a distorted and convoluted version of the truth.

The truth is not always easy on the ears. It will stop you from feeling certain ways. It will stop you from doing certain things you may really want to do. It will make you pause and reflect, think and fall on your face in awe of God. The anointing that rests on His Word will actually perk your ears up so that you begin to notice your own and other's genetically-altered views.

You'll start to hear them like *pow, pow, pow!* You don't ever have to be rude. You don't ever want to use the Word to bring division. If you do that, you are acting in a prideful spirit. Instead, you can hear anybody preach, anybody teach and get *something*...all while bypassing the genetically altered stuff. That's what I do and it brings me great peace.

I can learn from anyone. I can also dismiss genetically altered things from people I admire most. I may want to share what I know, but not to cut people—to help people. And if they don't believe it, so be it. God will sort it ALL out one day.

1 Corinthians 13:12-13 NKJV says, *"For now we see in a mirror, dimly, but then face to face. Now I know in part, but then I shall know just as I also am known. And now abide faith, hope, love, these three; but the greatest of these is love."*

In other words, one day we are all going to know things way more clearly than we do today, so why fight with one another? Above all we need to abide in love with one another.

## Watch Out for the Corners

It's kind of like when a child's running around the house. You may see the corner of the table coming before they ever do. If you have love in you, you'll try and warn them of that corner. Some will listen and others will keep on running. Some will be spared the hit and never get damaged by a blow. Others will hit that corner over and over again…and then cry and lament their situation, maybe way more than once.

What can you do? You can only share what you know with others so that they might be spared harm. You can try and touch their head even and guide them away from that fast-coming corner but if they don't listen, all you can do is pray for them. Pray that God gets through to them so that they don't have to experience that pain. And if they get hurt anyway, pray that His mercy will help them and His grace will be sufficient for them to make it through alright in the end.

I love it when God Himself reaches His hand around and grabs my head and helps me avoid the corner! He will do that, you know, through the Holy Spirit working in you. The more you are sensitive to His Holy Spirit, the greater His hand can guide you. The more you're in the flesh, the less you will see the corner coming.

I believe when we get to Heaven, we'll get to see all the times God stretched out His hand to help us—all the corners we *didn't* hit along the way in life. I think we'll be surprised and say, "Look, God! You just saved my life right there and I didn't even realize it! Thank you!!!"

# CHAPTER 24

# *They Laughed Then...*
# *But They Aren't Laughing Now*

People notice one thing really—manifestation. It doesn't matter what you say, but it's what you produce that people notice. You can talk about joy all day, but if you walk around sad all the time, why should anybody take what you say to heart? You get my point. You have to let your light shine.

I went into full-time ministry in 1978. Now, I'm liable to say anything behind the pulpit. I'm real and I will say what I think from time to time. My wife jokes, "Don't tell Jesse anything you don't want to hear from the pulpit!" The truth is, I will keep a person's secret private and it'll go to my grave—and, let me tell you this, there are *many* things only Jesus, me, and the person who told me know about. But if we're just talking fluff and nonsense, well, it's all fair game to me.

## Going Public With My Vision

When I was just starting out, I started to see the Lord changing me. He started leading me to say things that were totally out of my character—but they became a big part of my character as time marched on.

In the middle of a sermon, He would say, "Tell them you're going to build this!" I would think, *But, I don't want to do that God.* He wouldn't let up and He would say something to me like, "Tell them that *I* told you to build it." I would fight within myself, *I don't want to do that God. Let's just do that privately and I'll invite them when it's done.* He would refuse and say, "No, no! Tell them." So I would. And the things He had me profess that I would do shocked me, more than those who heard the words come out of my mouth.

What was He doing? Stretching me. Putting His hand out to guide me away from the walls and the corners, and into the big, free, wide-open plan of His will for my life. It totally changed me. It helped me to grow. Before, if I had an inkling of what God wanted me to do, I would say nothing—zero. If He told me to do something big, I didn't tell anyone. If God blessed me, nobody knew. One day, the Lord blessed me and then asked, "What's the matter? Are you embarrassed?" The truth was, I was embarrassed.

In those early years, it was very hard but whenever I did get blessed, I found myself making excuses for it. Things like, "Well, you know, I got this on sale" or "So and so gave this to me" and such.

I remember the Lord asking me, "What's wrong?"

"Well, Lord, if I start to say anything...it comes off kind of crass. You know, people think I'm cocky."

"What do you care what people think about you? Don't you care what I think about you?" He asked.

So, I began to branch out and tell people what God was doing for me—without excuses. I began to say, "This is what I'm going to build" or "God is going to give me this" or "God is going to do this for me." These were things that were way out of my league at the time—like debt-free buildings, jets, and worldwide television broadcasts. None of these things originated with me. All came by way of God talking to me about what He was going to do...but when I started telling people, they did just what I thought they would. They laughed.

## From Laughter to Name Calling

I was scorned and it hurt my feelings some. But it didn't hurt my feelings to the point of *offense* and it surely did not stop my faith. You see, I decided at some point to let the scorners do their thing, and to let God do His. I knew I wasn't crazy. I knew what God had said, and I chose to believe Him rather than let those who laughed me to scorn destroy my trust and faith in God.

Well, many years later, a lot of what I said in those early times came to pass...and the scorners stopped laughing straight in my face. Instead, they called me names. They considered me arrogant. They attacked my sermons and tried to make me feel small. But, I knew God was in charge.

I may be small in the flesh, but with God, I'm more than a conqueror—and I'm not about to let some intellectually lofty preacher make me feel less than what God called me to be. When God promotes, nobody can stop it. When He swings the door open, nobody can close it.

## Many Years Later

I'll never forget when I built Covenant Church, the local outreach of my ministry. Nearly twenty years had passed since I first began in ministry and since I first endured the scorn of others. Now, I had built Covenant Church and all the other ministry buildings completely debt-free—with cash money.

Today, I don't owe a dime on those buildings and it's a wonderful thing. It means I got what I paid for and not the typical three times the amount due to interest on 30 years of payments. I like to say I serve a Jewish God. He knows how to do business.

Now, nobody seems to do much debt-free, but I'm sticking with it. I don't care what others are doing. I have faith in God and I must do what He has told me to do—whether the whole world laughs or not.

The night we dedicated Covenant Church, I was shocked when some of the same preachers who had laughed me to scorn when I was just a young preacher came and sat in the pews to honor me. They stood up and applauded when I walked up to the pulpit. I almost passed out. You see, a lot of time had passed but I still remembered their harsh words to me.

The very same people who called me stupid...the same ones who said I was an idiot Cajun...the same ones who mocked my sermons as fluff and called me a court jester...the same ones who laughed when I talked about a jet to fly all over the world preaching the Gospel...the same ones who laughed at me and my wife for living in a 900 sq ft house so that we could put all the money into the new ministry...the same ones who said I couldn't build anything much less a bunch of buildings debt free—many of those *same* people were in the audience that night.

I had invited my friend to preach the dedication service and he told everyone there that night about the place being debt-free and said all sorts of nice things...and then, he had the whole crowd do something that I thought was amazing. He told everyone to get up out of the pews and walk to the walls of the sanctuary. "I want all of you to touch this holy place," he said. I couldn't believe it. He wanted the whole crowd, including those men who had laughed me to scorn, to get up and pray and touch the walls with their hands.

At first, nobody moved. They didn't seem to want to listen to the prophet of God who was speaking. Maybe they were just hesitating, not because of his odd request, but maybe because they were so shocked that we actually did it.

My friend said, "Is something wrong with y'all ears? Did you hear what I said? Get up, go to the wall." Well, up they all went. They prayed. They shouted. It was wonderful. And, when it was all over, people kept saying, "Can you believe Jesse actually did what he said and built this debt free? I can't believe he did it."

You see, there were lots of preachers in the room and preachers know what big bills are. Preachers build buildings all the time, and preachers get their churches and ministries in debt up to their eyeballs. Buildings cost millions of dollars. Television time costs even more—it's a money eating machine because the bills mount up every week. There is no payment plan. You pay for your time and, hey, rates are only going up on you.

When some of those preachers saw that what I'd said long ago I actually did, well, it was so big in their eyes, that they still could hardly believe it...yet they couldn't deny it either! They were sitting in a debt-free pew!

So, they said things to one another like, "I don't believe it. How can he do this? He's just a jokester. He's a Christian comedian." It was all the same, "He can't do that" and "He can't do this" even though I was doing all of that and this! Of course, people told me all these things they said afterward. Meanwhile, all during the service and after, I just kept smiling.

## *God Did It!*

In fact, there was this one man who was a really big preacher when I was starting out in ministry and he had really hurt me in the beginning. He came to that dedication service and when another one of my friends saw him sitting in the service, he told me, "Boy, Jesse, you ought to cut that sucker's guts out. He deserves it!"

My friend wanted me to say something, to call him out for all the things he had said about me for so many years. But, I'd learned better than that. My flesh may have wanted to do it, but my spirit was too light to clog it up with bitterness. So, instead, I had him stand up and I honored him in front of everyone. My friend later told me, "Boy, you know how to wash somebody's feet. I would have burned that sucker right there!"

The truth is that vengeance is God's alone. Yes, I'd have preferred it to be mine...years ago when the man was hurting me! But in the end, it's always His and if you honor God and His timing, He will honor you in due time.

I couldn't help but remember all those years back when I had no words to say except, "Lord?"...times when the hurt of other's words tried to stamp out my dreams and I couldn't help but remember His response to me so many years ago.

"Jesse," He said, "They always wanted to see something. So I'm gonna show them something."

God sure did that. He used *me*...and that was show enough for all of them.

## Faith Works, I'm Convinced!

Today, people accuse me of all sorts of new things. They say I'm only about money. That's not true, but I don't care what they say. Yes, I have money and plenty of it. Yes, I have a plane. Yes, I am debt-free. Yes, I'm on television. Yes, I travel and preach a lot of places. Yes, I've been in ministry from the time my hair was brown to now, when it is as white as snow...and yes, God is still using me and blessing me, and giving me favor.

I'm not lucky. I'm not that good either. My success has come because I've honored God—and I've done what He's told me to do, hell or high water. Faith works. I don't have to be convinced. I've seen it in action in my own life and ministry.

But, you know, even if I got nothing at all in life, I would still believe—because my experiences don't have to validate the Word of God. God stands alone. He needs no validation.

God is the Creator of the universe and the Creator of my soul. He is the One who will be left standing in the end. His adversary is beaten and doesn't realize it. God is eternal and He has made me eternal too—by way of salvation through the blood of His dear Son.

## What Is God's Will On Earth?

I'm going to live forever. When my body dies, I'm going to live in Heaven for eternity. So, I figure that I might as well start doing what He said now. I might as well have faith in Him now, right here on earth. Why wait until Heaven? It's better that I believe Him when I don't see Him, right? I aim to fulfill His Son's Words in the "Our

Father" prayer...I'm going to live out His will "in earth as it is in Heaven."

What is His will in Heaven? Sickness? Disease? Poverty? Bitterness? Lack? Misery? Backbiting? Strife? NO. It is the opposite of all that! It's health, prosperity, joy, nothing missing or broken, and unity with all the rest of my brothers and sisters in the faith!

I am a flesh man, but I want to live by the Spirit every day. I may not do everything right, but I am not aiming to do one thing wrong. If I fall, I will arise. If I fail, God will give me strength to get through it and grace to succeed the next time.

## Victory Is Ours...Period!

God will win in my life because He has already won—from the foundations of the earth, He won. He is the winner, no matter who fights Him. That makes me a winner too. So, no matter who laughs...no matter who attacks...no matter who scorns or fights me. The battle is the Lords, but the victory is mine. The victory is yours too. Period.

You see, in this life, you have to get yourself a foundation that won't crack under pressure—because this world is full of tribulation and pressure. There is always going to be somebody who wants to pollute your mind. There is always going to be something that wants to steal your will. There is always someone or something that's going to threaten to take what God has freely given to you.

Genetically altered Christianity is vanity and it's everywhere—don't let anybody distort the purity of your faith in God's Word. Jesus fought the devil's temptation with the pure, unadulterated, un-genetically altered, un-lofty intellectualized Word of God. That is what it will take for you to win and succeed too.

Don't be upset when you get scorned. Remember me...and remember that God always has the last laugh. Let His Word remain true and pure in you. Use it with child-like faith and *watch* what He will do. It may not be tomorrow, or next month or next year but His Word to you *will* come to pass...and it will keep on coming to pass for eternity.

God's Word is real, raw, pure and forever. Don't accept a genetically altered substitute. Have faith in the real thing and stick with God. You're going to win!

# Prayer of Salvation

A born-again, committed relationship with God is the key to the victorious life. Jesus, the Son of God, laid down His life and rose again so that we could spend eternity with Him in Heaven and experience His absolute best on earth. The Bible says, *"For God so loved the world, that he gave his only begotten Son, that whosoever believeth in him should not perish, but have everlasting life"* (John 3:16).

It is the will of God that everyone receive eternal salvation. The way to receive this salvation is to call upon the name of Jesus and confess Him as your Lord. The Bible says, *"That if thou shalt confess with thy mouth the Lord Jesus, and shalt believe in thine heart that God hath raised him from the dead, thou shalt be saved. For whosoever shall call upon the name of the Lord shall be saved"* (Romans 10:9-10,13).

Jesus has given salvation, healing, and countless benefits to all who call upon His name. These benefits can be yours if you receive Him into your heart by praying this prayer:

*Heavenly Father, I come to You admitting that I am a sinner. Right now, I choose to turn away from sin, and I ask You to cleanse me of all unrighteousness. I believe that Your Son, Jesus, died on the cross to take away my sins. I also believe that He rose again from the dead so that I may be justified and made righteous through faith in Him. I call upon the name of Jesus Christ to be the Savior and Lord of my life. Jesus, I choose to follow You, and I ask that You fill me with the power of the Holy Spirit. I declare that right now, I am a born-again child of God. I am free from sin and full of the righteousness of God. I am saved in Jesus' name, Amen.*

If you have prayed this prayer to receive Jesus Christ as your Savior, or if this book has changed your life, we would like to hear from you. Please contact us at:

**Jesse Duplantis Ministries**
PO Box 1089
Destrehan, LA 70047

985.764.2000
**www.jdm.org**

# About the Author

Jesse Duplantis is what some would call a true evangelist. Supernaturally saved and delivered from a life of addiction in 1974 and called by God to the office of the evangelist in 1978, he founded Jesse Duplantis Ministries with one mission in his mind and one vision in his heart—global evangelism, whatever the cost. And throughout his many years of evangelistic ministry, he has sought to do just that.

With a television ministry that spans the globe, ministry offices in America, the United Kingdom, and Australia, and a preaching itinerary that has taken him to thousands of different churches to date, Jesse is still fulfilling his original call to evangelism with gusto! His commitment to Christ, long-standing integrity in ministry, and infectious, joyful nature have made him one of the most loved and respected ministers of the gospel today. Oral Roberts Ministries recognized his achievements in the field of evangelism by awarding him an honorary doctorate of divinity in 1999.

A Cajun from Southern Louisiana, Jesse makes the Bible easy to understand by preaching its truths in our everyday vernacular and spicing his messages with humor. Often called the "Apostle of Joy" because of hilarious illustrations, Jesse's anointed preaching and down-to-earth style have helped to open the door for countless numbers of people to receive Jesus as their Lord and Savior. Jesse has proven through his own life that no matter who you are or where you come from, God can change your heart, develop your character through His Word, and help you find and complete your divine destiny.

To contact Jesse Duplantis Ministries,
write or call:

Jesse Duplantis Ministries
PO Box 1089
Destrehan, LA 70047
985.764.2000
www.jdm.org

*Please include your prayer requests, praise reports
and comments when you write.*

# Other Books by Jesse Duplantis

The Everyday Visionary

What in Hell Do You Want?

Wanting A God You Can Talk To

Breaking the Power of Natural Law

Jambalaya for the Soul
Heaven—Close Encounters of the God Kind
*Also available in Spanish*

God Is Not Enough, He's Too Much!

The Ministry of Cheerfulness

The Sovereignty of God

Running Toward Your Giant

Don't Be Affected by the World's Message

Keep Your Foot on the Devil's Neck

Leave It in the Hands of a Specialist

One More Night With the Frogs

The Battle of Life

Understanding Salvation
*Also available in Spanish*


Available at your local bookstore.